Familiar Territory

Familiar Territory

OBSERVATIONS ON AMERICAN LIFE

JOSEPH EPSTEIN

New York   Oxford
OXFORD UNIVERSITY PRESS
1979

Copyright © 1979 by Joseph Epstein

Library of Congress Cataloging in Publication Data
Epstein, Joseph, 1937– Familiar territory.
1. National characteristics, American—Addresses, essays, lectures.
2. United States—Civilization—1970–   —Addresses, essays, lectures. I. Title.
E169.12.E67   973.92   79-10150   ISBN 0-19-502604-7

The lines from *And Even Now* by Max Beerbohm are reprinted by permission of Mrs. Eva Reichmann.

The lines from *The People, Yes* by Carl Sandburg are reprinted by permission of Harcourt Brace Jovanovich, Inc.

'The Jogger's Prayer" © Tom Wolfe, 1978, is reprinted by permission of Tom Wolfe.

The lines from "Sunday Morning": Copyright 1923 and renewed 1951 by Wallace Stevens. Reprinted from *The Collected Poems of Wallace Stevens* by permission of Alfred A. Knopf, Inc.

Printed in the United States of America

To Barbara,
Best Friend and Wife

Preface

All the essays in this book originally appeared in *The American Scholar*. When I first became editor of that journal, in 1974, I had no intention of writing for it regularly. What I had intended was to set up a column that members of the journal's Editorial Board could avail themselves of to shoot off opinions, speculations, or oddly angled views that might not be so easily contained in formal essays of the traditional kind. I wrote the first of these essays, which I signed with the pseudonym Aristides, after Aristides the Just, the early fifth century Athenian leader who was finally ostracized by the citizens of Athens because they grew tired of always hearing him called the Just. Happily, nobody chose to step in to write the second essay, so I wrote that one too; and I have been writing them ever since, one every three months, for the past five years.

As for the essays themselves, they are of the kind known as "familiar." The familiar essay has a long and distinguished tradition, going back to Addison and Steele in England and even further back to Montaigne in France. William Hazlitt and Charles Lamb were none too bad at the familiar essay either. Joseph Wood Krutch, who himself wrote such essays, defined the genre well, I think, when he wrote that "the familiar essay affords what is probably the best method of discussing those subjects which are neither obviously momentous nor merely silly." Another way of saying this is to say that the familiar essayist lives, and takes his professional sustenance, in the everyday flow of things. Familiar is his style and familiar, too, is the territory he writes about.

The one thing a familiar essayist must have is a point of view. By a point of view I do not mean a collection of opinions, which is a very different thing. Everyone has opinions—some correct, some incorrect—but not everyone has a point of view: a standpoint, a perspective, from which to view the world going on about him. If a writer has no real point of view, the familiar essay, if he writes more than a few of them, will soon develop one in him. This is not to say that he must come to every subject with a locked-in view of it. Very often the familiar essayist—or at least this one— does not know what he thinks until he has finished writing about it. But without a point of view he has no subject at all.

With a point of view all but the most recondite subjects belong to the familiar essayist, whose range is precisely as wide as his interests. He is in this respect rather like Carlyle's Professor Teufelsdröch, a Professor of Things in General. I must say that since I have begun writing these essays I have never felt pressed for a subject; and so long as I continue to write them, I suspect I never shall be pressed. Part of this has to do with America. Rich in so many things, America is richest of all in things to write about. For the familiar essayist in America every day is like Christmas morning in a wealthy and loving Christian home; subjects, like gifts, are strewn about everywhere.

In the end the true job of the familiar essayist is to write what is on his mind and in his heart in the hope that, in doing so, he will say what others have sensed only inchoately. Apart from the writing itself, his keenest pleasure comes when someone says to him, "I read your essay on television (food, jokes, language, etc.); you have said what I have always felt." How often the essays in this book will accomplish this is for their readers not for their author to say. But when it does happen, it is like calling out in the desert and having a voice answer back. At such times above all others does the familiar essay breed content.

J.E.

Contents

Familiar Territory

Greetings and Salutations

It is not, I recognize, a social problem of the order of seriousness of public housing or drug addiction, but to me, because I am more than a trifle literal-minded, it has long seemed vexing. How to begin a letter and how to end one, how to open a conversation and how to close one—simple enough matters of manners, one might have thought—have come to be a cause for consternation. "Manners are morals in bloom," reports a nineteenth-century authority on etiquette. My own garden, alas, is looking rather sickly.

My problem is not altogether a formal one, although, reading up on the subject, I find my formal ignorance is considerable. On the item of letter writing I recently discovered how considerable it is by consulting that treasure house of information on the subject, Emily Post's *Etiquette*, in the 1965 edition revised by Mrs. Post's daughter-in-law, Elizabeth L. Post. I like the Mesdames Post, sometimes for the unconscious humor to be found in their pages, but also because they are women of strong and clear character who have, as John Sparrow once put it in another context, the courage of their conventions.

A dip into *Etiquette* never, for me, fails to provide a fresh

3

discovery. On my last such immersion, for example, I learned that my wife is not allowed to use my crest on her letter paper, for, say the Posts, "the crest is the exclusive property of male members of a family." "Surprisingly few Americans," write the Posts, whose capacity for astonishment far exceeds my own, "seem to be aware of this heraldic rule."

Sisyphean are the labors of those who would codify manners at any time, but the stone is especially slippery in our own time. Manners have been properly defined as the overt forms of social intercourse that, when conventionalized, ease personal relationships. But the problem nowadays is that they rarely are allowed time to become conventional. New wine in new wine bottles is the American way. Often this has comic results. If I read them aright, the Mrs. Posts maintain it to be good form for a divorced woman, in her correspondence, to retain her married name and append to it her maiden name. Thus the former Mary Johnson, having married and divorced Robert Simpson—with impeccable manners, the Posts refuse to go into the reasons for the divorce— would be correctly addressed as Mrs. Simpson Johnson. My edition of the Posts' *Etiquette* was brought out in 1965, or before the rise of the new feminism. What if the former Mary Johnson were an ardent feminist (which might, by the way, throw some light on the divorce)? If she were, like as not she would insist that her married name be, as the Irish say, parted in the middle by a hyphen, making her Mary Johnson-Simpson. After she left poor Simpson, would it be *de rigueur* to address future correspondence to her as Mrs. Johnson-Simpson Johnson? You see the quandary.

In other questions of etiquette, the arrangements of the new feminism seem to have caused as many problems as they have solved. Take the neologism *Ms.*, which, whatever the political impetus behind it, might have been supposed at least to have solved the technical problem of addressing letters to women whose marital status was uncertain. Whether one likes Ms. or not—and Graham Greene, among others, has registered public distaste for it on the grounds that it is unpronounceable—it does promise a certain efficiency. Courtesy here would seem to call for addressing people as they wish to be addressed; if women wish to be addressed as Ms., Negroes as blacks, West Coast Mexican-Americans as Chicanos, this is fair and easily enough accommodated. But many women, it turns out, despise being addressed as Ms.; some are pleased to have it known they are single, others proud of being married. The late novelist Jean Stafford once remarked that to her the letters MS would everlastingly stand for manuscript or multiple sclerosis. When letters addressed to Ms. Jean Stafford arrived, she returned them unread, first opening them—a nice practical touch—to see if they contained a check.

Other advents of decorum owing to feminism make for further social touchiness. The use of the suffix "person," as in "chairperson," appears to rile fully as many people as it delights. Much depends, of course, on whose mouth the new phrases come out of. I have by experience been made a bit wary of men who too exuberantly rush into this practice. My first encounter with the greeting "Dear Gentlepersons" was not a happy one. No gentle person himself, its user followed up his letter with a telephone call to a female co-worker of mine in which he proved so bullying as to bring her near to tears. When he asked to speak with me, he said, "Mr. Epstein, may I ask you a question? Are you a person who is flexible and open to innovation, or closed-minded and rigid?" I replied, "Closed-minded and rigid," which put *paid* to that conversation. But ever since, I have warned women to beware letters addressed to them as "Dear Gentleperson." They may come from a rapist.

Another problem has nothing to do with feminism but with what I think of as the regulation of intimacy in a correspondence. This cuts two ways: how to keep at bay those with whom one does not wish to extend the line of informal-

ity, and how to gain greater intimacy with those one wishes
to know better. I speak of the great first-name problem. Autobiographical experience here, too, has not always been fe-
licitous. In Chicago, the city of my birth and upbringing,
policemen, or at least some of them, after stopping one for a
traffic violation and requesting one's driver's license, were
fond of beginning, "Well, I guess you know you were speed-
ing, Joseph." Such enforced (and one-way) intimacy was
generally a signal for a bribe. Salesmen, too—usually those
whose pressure sends the mercury flying up toward the top
of the thermometer—are often quick with first names.

"I think we have exactly the car you want, sir. Now, if you
will take a seat here, we'll first run over the figures. Can I
have your name, sir?"

"Epstein."

"First name, sir."

"The initial is J."

"Can I have the full name, sir, for our records?"

"Joseph."

"Great. Well, now, did you want the factory air and the
radial tires on this baby, Joe?"

In correspondence, being wary of growing too quickly intimate with those I have never met, I find myself almost as
wary of those who wish too quickly to become intimate with
me. Either a natural diffidence or an unnatural stiffness
causes me to be put off by letters or telephone calls from
persons I have never been in touch with before who come on
with my first name. Men and women of the media, who
apparently feel themselves right at home everywhere, seem
to have the habit of instant intimacy. On the infrequent occasions when I am invited by phone to appear on a radio or
television talk show and a stranger calls me by my first
name, I generally ask as quickly as possible what he will pay
me to appear on the show. When he says—as they invariably
do—that budget does not allow payments to guests, I then
ask if he would consider giving me a portion of his salary,

since by appearing on the show I should be helping him earn it. "What, incidentally," I will ask, if in a sufficiently mischievous mood, "do you earn per week?" If you wish to be intimate, this question is calculated to imply, then let's *really* get intimate. Oddly enough, it immediately lends a cold air of formality to further conversation.

True intimacy is not only a many-splendored but a subtle thing—and progressing toward it in a correspondence can be a matter of great delicacy. Sometimes one's wish for greater intimacy is simply out of one's control to act upon. If one's correspondent is much older, or by general recognition more distinguished, or (in what is sometimes necessarily a political context) more powerful, then the lead toward intimacy is his rather than one's own. (Not for me to have addressed a letter to the late T. S. Eliot "Dear Tom," yet how pleasing it would have been to have had him address one to me as "Dear Joe"!) But in a correspondence between two persons who are, roughly speaking, equals, things can grow trickier. The tone of the letters generally gives the clue, although sometimes the duration of the correspondence can make reverting to first names permissible.

Among intellectuals and academics, frequently there is a gradation in the steps from surnames to first names in which both names are pressed into service: thus, "Dear Joseph Epstein"; or, in the same gradation, making use of the diminutive first name: "Dear Joe Epstein." Many people are put off by this use of both one's names, and I am among them, although I cannot say exactly why. Perhaps it smacks too much of memories of grade-school scoldings: "Joseph Epstein, you march down to the principal's office this moment!" It is also too betwixt-and-between, an odious and/or—neither formal nor intimate but rather like wearing a dinner jacket with tennis shoes.

The best solution I have seen to this problem was that adopted by an Englishman whom I have known only through letters, but whom I have come to think of as a friend. When our correspondence began, we shared mutual acquaintances and common interests. As the correspondence picked up, it became clear that our senses of humor were similar as well. The initial reason for our exchange of letters was business, and the first three or four of his letters, along with being about business, ended on a light and witty note. He began what was perhaps the fifth in our exchange of letters with the following opening: "Dear Mr. Epstein, I do wish that, as Henry James once wrote under comparable circumstances, I could 'take a flying leap at the barrier of formality' and use your first name." That may be too literary for some tastes, but not for mine. More than two years later, I still marvel at the immense courtesy of that beginning. A delightful step in a dance to the music of friendship, it provided a lead wonderfully easy to follow. "Dear John," I was easily able to reply in my next letter to him, "There now, Henry James's barrier of formality is leapt." Manners so elegant go far beyond etiquette to become what manners at their best always are—the kindliest consideration for others.

Ever a fount of new knowledge, Emily and Elizabeth Post inform me that the opening "My dear Miss X" is more formal than "Dear Miss X," cascading down, in degrees of informality and toward greater intimacy, to "Dear Sally," "Sally dear," "Dearest Sally," "Sally darling," and ending doubtless in outright obscenities of intimacy. Yet European men, I note, often address letters to another man with "My dear," followed by one's last name alone: "My dear Epstein." Perhaps it is another instance of America's slavishly following Europe, but I find something dashing and manly in such an opening. It has about it the hurried quality of the man of affairs shooting off a quick communication from (say) the Finland Station, or exile, or the battlefront.

In my own correspondence, because I am a sometime university teacher, I find myself often misaddressed as Dr. Epstein—misaddressed because I have no doctorate and am thus undeserving of the academicizing prefix. Explaining this is usually too complicated, so I let it ride. Among academics, scientists seem, in my experience, to go in for this doctoring of one another more than do those in the social sciences or the humanities. The initials Ph.D. after one's signature continue to be put to use by many men and women at smaller or backwater colleges and universities; possibly for this reason, "Dr." has come to seem rather bush league. Whenever the voice at the other end of the telephone—often a student but sometimes a nonacademic—begins by asking, "Is this Dr. Epstein?" I find myself having to fight back the temptation to respond, "It is. My advice is read two chapters of Flaubert and get right into bed."

But I should prefer, any day, to be misaddressed as "Dr." than in what I have come to think of as the style of the contemptuous familiar. Possibly deriving from the old cockney use of "Guvnor," behind which I am not sure there was any malice, in the United States the contemptuous familiar variants have tended to take a nastier turn. Once in greater use than now by cabdrivers, bus drivers, bartenders, and roughhouse clerks, the main terms of the contemptuous familiar used to be Mac, Ace, Chief, Buddy, Skipper, Speedy, and Tiger. ("Where to, Mac?" "What's yours, Ace?" "More coffee, Chief?") The equivalent terms for women in the contemptuous familiar were Sister, Sweetheart, Baby, and Doll. For reasons I do not quite understand, the contemptuous familiar seems to be passing from the scene, leaving merely free-floating contempt in its wake.

As a form of greeting, handshaking as well has undergone change. Thirty years ago and more, a firm handshake, at least between men, was considered a mark of masculinity and even something of a key to male character; or so, at any rate, young boys were instructed by their fathers. ("Don't give a man a dead fish, son. Squeeze a man's hand.") No longer, I suspect. Two, and possibly more, new styles of handshake have come into vogue. The first, on display regularly in televised sports events, is the slap downward on the palm-upward hand. ("Can I get it, Baby?" Slap. "You got it.") This has a certain utility when, for example, a baseball player crosses the plate after a homer and is greeted there by several teammates. The other new handshake is a more Roman affair. Instead of hands being extended and meeting out away from the body, they are joined more vertically, as if in the beginning position for hand wrestling. The first time I had this new handshake used on me, I extended my hand for my traditional square handshake, whereupon my arm was jerked upward, my fingers locked in a tight grasp, and I barely averted going down for the count.

The Posts offer advice aplenty, along with models, on the kinds of letters to write in response to specific occasions, but I am afraid that I am inaccessible to their sensible advice. The reason is that some years ago I read a little parody on the subject of model letters entitled "How Shall I Word It?" by Max Beerbohm, which has made such advice forever laughable to me, as it would to anyone who came across it. Here is Max Beerbohm's model letter in acknowledgment of a wedding present:

> Dear Lady Amblesham,
>   Who gives quickly, says the old proverb, gives twice. For this reason I have purposely delayed writing to you, lest I should appear to thank you more than once for the small, cheap, hideous present you sent me on the occasion of my recent wedding. Were you a poor woman, that little bowl of ill-imitated Dresden china would convict you of tastelessness merely; were you a blind woman, of nothing but an odious parsimony. As you have normal eyesight and more than normal wealth, your gift to me proclaims you at once a Philistine and a miser (or rather did so proclaim you until, less than ten seconds after I unpacked it from its wrappings of tissue paper, I took it to the open

window and had the satisfaction of seeing it shat-
tered to atoms on the pavement). But stay! I perceive a possible flaw in my argument. Perhaps you
were guided in your choice by a definite wish to
insult me. I am sure, on reflection, that this was
so. *I shall not forget.*

Yours, etc.,
Cynthia Beaumarsh

PS My husband asks me to tell you to warn Lord
Amblesham to keep out of his way or to assume
some disguise so complete that he will not be recognized by him and horsewhipped.

PPS I am sending copies of this letter to the principal London and provincial newspapers.

Which brings me to what, in the letter-writing manuals, is
charmingly called the "complimentary close." Once the closing of a letter was itself an act of delicate art, comparable to
the coda of a symphonic work. To find a transition that
smoothly linked the body of a letter to its close was a problem every gracious letter writer had to confront: ". . . your
many kindnesses to me, who remains, and shall everlastingly, your most humble and obedient servant. Yours
&c. . . ." Today we are left to sign off with a single word or
phrase that is supposed to embody the sentiments of all that
has gone before, be it "Sincerely" or "Truly" or "Cordially"
or "Faithfully" or sending along "Best wishes." But what
about those literal-minded letter writers among us who feel
that neither sincerity nor truthfulness nor cordiality nor
faithfulness quite describes us? Sometimes I, for one, feel
"Affectionately" toward those to whom I write, but not by a
long shot to everyone. I could, I suppose, sign myself "As
ever" but for the fact that I am so changeable in my moods.
To sign myself "Tentatively" will not do, and I frankly wish
to reserve my "Best wishes" for my immediate family. The
position of people like me is akin to that of Mr. Llewellyn

Hutchinson, who, after many years of not being able to get a letter printed in *The Times* (London)—"the duty of the distinguished," as one correspondent put it, ". . . ever the ambition of the obscure"—wrote to that august journal on January 11, 1930:

> Sir,
>   Like your correspondent "Victorian," I do not address you as "Dear Sir," because you are not dear to me, unless you print my letter. But I decline to accept "Victorian's" dictum that I must sign myself "always" (or even for a moment) "your obedient servant." I cannot tell a lie, with any chance of success, and I am *not* your obedient servant. I do not believe that "Victorian" would remain your obedient servant if you told him not to write to you any more. "Yours, &c." is horrible; "yours sincerely" is insincere; "yours truly" is untrue. "Yours faithfully" seems to hit the mark. We obscure persons who write to you are full of Faith: so full, in fact, that there is no room for Hope.
>
>   Yours faithfully,
>   Llewellyn Hutchinson

H. L. Mencken, painted into a corner by his own brash iconoclasm, had a similar problem. Not for him the easy use of "Sincerely," "Truly," or "Cordially." As a famous agnostic, he would frequently end his letters by offering to pray for his correspondent. To letters violently attacking his writings, he would rejoin, on a preprinted postcard, "Dear Sir or Madame: You may or may not be right." In some of his letters, in a single-phrase criticism of the entire project of closing a letter, he would sign off, "All the usual hypocrisies."

Of course, social intercourse has need of little hypocrisies, the more usual the better, to lubricate and thus smooth the way to more important things. Best to look upon them as stage instructions, ways of getting one's own character on and off the stage. One's entrances and exits are not, after all, as significant as what is said on the stage itself. Yet too discordant a note coming onstage can foul the main dialogue, and too false a note upon exiting can have a similar result. In conversation, either in person or over the telephone, "Hello" and "Good-bye" might be thought sufficient, but most of us seek, in our greetings and farewells, a trademark expressive of what we deem to be special about our personalities. Possibly this is modeled on show-business figures and radio and television broadcasters, most of whom have devised their own particular ways of signing off.

"Take care," "Take it easy," "Take it easy—but do take it," "Be good," "Peace," "Shalom," "*Ciao*," and, more recently, "Take it light" (as opposed, one gathers, to taking it heavy)—these are among the standard conversational closes of our day. Sometimes a regional twist will be added. In the South, upon departing a shop or someone's home, it is not uncommon to be sent off with, "Hurry on back now, y'hear?" Generally, this causes me to wish I could go out the door, then come right back in, set down my carpetbag, and announce, "Well, as per your instructions, here I am again."

Still another fairly new salute upon departure has arisen: "Have a good day." I once thought that this was indigenous to the Middle West, but of late I have heard it said with fair frequency on both coasts. "Have a good day" is apparently another of those expressions that have the power of getting under people's skin. Some deplore it with sufficient fervor to allow its utterance to ruin their day altogether. Years ago, when someone would say "Nice day" to Henry Luce, not the most easygoing of men, he would, according to his biographer W. A. Swanberg, shoot back, "Why do you say that?" Why do so many people now say "Have a good day"? It fills the gap at the end of conversation or business dealings; it offers a gentle way offstage; it provides a harmless mode of well-wishing; it has a pleasant rhythm.

Yet "Have a good day" raises certain questions. Why merely a good day? Why not a good week? Or month? Or indeed fiscal year? I myself could use a good decade. A witty television sports broadcaster named Ray Gandoff used to end his broadcasts by saying, "Have a good life," which is perhaps getting too much into the spirit of the thing. What is decisive, and easily enough judged, is the feeling behind "Have a good day." Over the radio a woman who has just learned that she has lost $10,000 dollars for not answering her phone by saying "WMAQ is going to make me rich," says: "Oh, my God! How terrible!" "Too bad," the disc jockey informs her, "but maybe we'll call again. Meanwhile, have a good day." Fat chance.

Does any of this matter? In *The People, Yes* Carl Sandburg wrote:

> The people is Everyman, everybody.
> Everybody is you and me and all the others.
> What everybody says is what we all say.
> And what is it we all say?

Well, we all say pretty much the same thing. And yet each of us likes to distinguish himself—if not by his deeds, at least by his language. Some of us go in for precision, others for rhythm, still others for whatever is the going thing. Those of us who claim to care about language have a debt, an obligation to look for those forms of expression that have become petrified, those phrases that have become deadened, those mannerisms that have become hollow. I, at any rate, believe this an important task, and I believe it sincerely, truly, faithfully, respectfully, cordially, and affectionately. If you do not believe that it matters at all—well, what I wish to say to you is, "Have a good day."

State of the Lingo

Can you imagine the stir it would have caused had either of the candidates in the last presidential campaign pledged, if elected, to inaugurate a Department of Language with a Secretary of Language at its head? I can imagine the stir. It would, I think, have been nonexistent. Yet why not such a department? A nation's language, after all, is on the order of a natural resource—subject, like the others, to depletion, the ravages of pollution, thoughtless neglect. If such a department were to come into being, future presidents, somewhere toward the conclusion of their state of the union messages, might be able to report: "The Secretary of Language has informed me that over the past year our strength in verbs has not in any way diminished, adjectives of great pungency are being developed in the Northwest, and for the first time in decades profanity has become interesting once again." Alas, we are not soon likely to hear such messages about the state of the American language, even though, as anyone who has thought about it will agree, the American language appears to be in quite a state.

The notion of a Department of Language—or, more modestly, an American Academy like unto the French Academy in its function of, to quote the royal edict establishing it, working "with all the care and all the diligence possible at giving sure rules to our language, and rendering it pure, eloquent, and capable of treating the arts and sciences"—is one with a long, though not consistently distinguished, history in the United States. John Adams was perhaps the first to propose such an academy for the United States when he wrote from abroad in 1780 suggesting an academy be set up for "correcting, improving, and ascertaining the English language." In England, another country without an academy, Matthew Arnold wrote about the benefits such institutions can confer in connection with "the *ethical* influences of style in language—its close relations, so often pointed out, with character," though adding that "such an effort to set up a recognized authority, imposing on us a high standard in matters of intellect and taste, has many enemies in human nature." In the United States the banner was soon picked up by lesser people than Adams and Arnold; it was picked up by the dry-as-dust pedagogues and by the schoolmarms; the crusaders for purity of the kind that H. L. Mencken so loved to castigate. "In 1915," he wrote in *The American Language*, "the National Council of Teachers of English, following that hopeful American custom which gave the nation Mothers' Day, and Safety-First, Paint-Up-Clean-Up, and Eat-More-Cheese Weeks, proposed to make the first seven days of November Better-Speech Week." Mencken is probably correct; the crusade for purity of language, or at least for correctness, is doubtless lost because of the nature of the crusaders. Careful language has had a bad press.

But greater difficulties are involved in establishing an American Academy, and chief among them would be selecting the people to serve on such a body. In the composition of the recently published *Harper's Dictionary of Contemporary Usage*, the volume's authors, William and Mary Morris, used the assistance of a 136-member panel of "prominent writers, editors, public speakers, educators, and commentators."

This is too great a number by far. In fact, I have recently noted that one of their panelists, Shana Alexander, in a letter to the *New York Times Book Review* in connection with a review of a book by Betty Friedan, writes that it seems to her "all the paranoia is on the other foot"—a condition that would appear to call for a podiatrist with psychiatric training. No, any Department of Language or Academy for the American Language would require people with clearer minds and more careful pens than that.

Most useful would it be to have someone noted for stringency in matters linguistical, someone as stringent as the late Edmund Wilson, who used to take time out, even when reviewing books he generally admired, to apply the corrective bastinado. Here is Wilson doing his necessary chore in a review of a work by George Kennan, himself the most elegant of prose writers among our diplomats and a man who has given ample evidence of caring about how language is used:

> Mr. Kennan, though so careful a scholar, with so fine an appreciation of literature, is in some ways rather careless as a writer. He habitually uses *transpire* as if it meant occur and *disinterestedness* as if it meant *lack of interest*. He makes "a series of demands" plural and uses wrongly a plural "protagonists" (you can have only one protagonist in any given situation). He writes, "The country was *rampant* with hardship and disease" and "He finally succeeded . . . in licking the heavy financial problem which the depression had *spelled* for the German government. . . ." It may well be that Mr. Kennan, with his new official duties, had not time to attend to these matters, but his publishers ought to have done so. They have left Mr. Kennan's expression sometimes limping behind his intellect.

Along with the tough-mindedness of an Edmund Wilson, generosity of a kind is also wanted for an American Acad-

emy. The generosity of H. L. Mencken, for example, whose
love of colorful slang and useful neologisms runs through the
pages of *The American Language*. Mencken, that so often contradictory man, made his mark ridiculing the "booboisie,"
yet ended his days praising "the national fancy for the terse,
the vivid, and, above all, the bold and imaginative" in language. In a footnote in *The Decline and Fall of the Roman
Empire* Gibbon remarks: "There is room for a very interesting work, which should lay open the connection between the
languages and manners of nations." In *The American Language* H. L. Mencken produced precisely such a book for the
United States.

Mencken was without linguistic snobbery, even though in
his own writing he sported a vocabulary rife, as he might
put it, with rococosities. Good linguistic sense he had in
plenty. Fending off the British attack on American "barba-
risms," he wrote in *The American Language*: "*Movie* is better
than *cinema*; and the English begin to admit the fact by
adopting the word; it is not only better American, it is better
English. *Bill-board* is better than *hoarding*. *Office-holder* is
more honest, more picturesque, more thoroughly Anglo-
Saxon than *public-servant*." Yet Mencken also styled himself
a "specialist in morbid philology." He was, in this connection, a good man with the literary knout, which he was prepared to lay on liberally when confronted with a pretentious
style. His likening the prose style of Warren G. Harding to "a
rhinoceros liberating himself by main strength from a lake
of boiling molasses" is unforgettable.

The membership of the French Academy is limited to
forty; ten might do for an American Academy, though it is
doubtful that even ten members could be found whose authority would go undisputed. They would have to be chosen
without regard to the niceties of affirmative action or to-
kenism of any sort. The kind of person who would qualify
would probably not be interested, simply because he would
recognize the task to be nearly a full-time one. The job at

hand, after all, would be essentially constabulary; not still another honorific body, but a linguistic police force, would be required.

The fact is that things have not quite worked out for our language as its friends have prophesied. Walt Whitman's ecstatic prediction about the English language in America is not coming true: "The Americans are going to be the most fluent and melodious voiced people in the world—and the most perfect users of words." From the other shore, Virginia Woolf wrote in 1925: "The Americans are doing what the Elizabethans did—they are coining new words. They are instinctively making the language adapt itself to their needs." Alas, would it were still so. That last sentence of Virginia Woolf's, for instance, edited for a contemporary American audience of the college-educated, would read: "The thrust of internal pressure deriving from new lifestyles is causing alterations in linguistic patterns to comply with national felt needs that are ongoing."

Resisting change is not at issue. "The essence of language," Otto Jespersen long ago and truly wrote, "is activity." About this point no dispute is possible. New words come in, old words go out; and in the verbal traffic of the United States it is always rush hour. There is nothing for it, except regret when a good word gets lost and distaste when a bad word is discovered. When a good word departs, it departs alone; but a bad word seems to send for relatives soon after its arrival. Thus that atrociously bad word "lifestyle" has brought in its train the equally atrocious "lifestance"; and from the other side of the family we now have "mindstyles" (a man named Nathaniel Lande has published a book entitled *Mindstyles / Lifestyles*), and, in the September 1976 issue of *Esquire*, the phrase "differing life and speech styles" crops up. Can birthstyle and death-stance be far behind?

Calling words "good" and "bad," though plain talk, is also moral talk. In his essay "The Literary Influence of Academies," Matthew Arnold spoke of "freaks" in dealing with language, noting that they "tend to impair the power and the beauty of language." For an example Arnold cited nothing more heinous than the *Times* of London's regularly misspelling the word "diocese" as "diocess." "Some people," he writes, "will say these are little things; they are not; they are of bad example. They tend to spread the baneful notion that there is no such thing as a high correct standard in intellectual matters; that everyone may as well take his own way; they are at variance with the severe discipline necessary for all real culture; they confirm us in habits of willfulness and eccentricity, which hurt our minds, and damage our credit with serious people."

By now, of course, things have gone well beyond the orthographic antics mentioned by Matthew Arnold. Reality is at issue, as is the capacity of words to capture it. The objection to the word "lifestyle" is that it is at too many removes from reality; in its contemporary usage is implied a number of assumptions about life that are belied by experience. Chief among these is an assumption about the absolute plasticity of character—change your lifestyle, change your life—that is simply not true; and the popularity of the word "lifestyle" is testimony to how much people want to believe it. One criterion for a bad word, then, is that it is too distant from reality.

Another criterion for badness is vagueness, especially a word or phrase that seems to promise a great deal and delivers very little. The slang phrases "putting it all together" and "getting it all together" are examples. I recall once asking a class how it would define success; the words money, fame, or power did not arise in response. Instead one student said that "success is a way of putting it all together." Ah, but could he describe what "it" might look like when once assembled? He could not. The same sort of vagueness infests another slang phrase: "He's (or she's) got his head screwed on straight." One senses a certain seriousness attributed to the person about whom this is said, but what I should still like to know is in which direction his newly screwed down head is facing.

Then there are crock words. A word that has no real meaning at all is essentially—to use a good new slang word—a "crock." Atop the list of words with no real meaning is "meaningful." Jimmy Carter has told us, through the journalism of Norman Mailer, that his major prayer is: "Let me live my life so that it will be meaningful." Mailer, in writing about Carter for the *New York Times Magazine,* was greatly taken by that. But whatever can Carter have meant by meaningful? Hitler was meaningful, so was Gandhi, and Attila the Hun, and Jesus Christ, and Josef Stalin, and Saint Francis of Assisi. What Carter means only God knows, but since he is using the word in a prayer, perhaps that is sufficient. Crock words generally come in various lengths and degrees of difficulty, and they tend to be more popular among literary men than among sociologists. Norman Mailer's "sensuous silence" is a crock phrase of some simplicity; and "the deconstructed self," a coinage of the literary critic Leo Bersani, is a crock that runneth over.

Other criteria for bad words are available. Some words are intrinsically ugly: the phrase "psychic mobility" has the look of being surrounded by barbed wire, placed there to keep out understanding. Other words are used with a boring repetitiveness, such as what I have come to think of as the "California Hey." This is the tendency of a great many people under fifty to begin all sentences with the word "Hey," serving in effect as an exclamation point, as in "Hey, who was that fine lady I saw you with last night?" But by far the greatest number of bad words and phrases qualify under the criteria set down above: they are removed from reality, they are vague, they are without meaning.

Whence does this shabby language derive? In 1906 Henry James, in *The American Scene,* under the rubric "The Fate of the Language," remarked upon his " 'lettered' anguish . . .

for the linguistic tradition as one had known it." He concluded: "The accent of the very ultimate future, in the States, may be destined to become the most beautiful on the globe and the very music of humanity (here the 'ethnic' synthesis shrouds itself thicker than ever); but whatever we shall know it for, certainly, we shall not know it for English—in any sense for which there is an existing literary measure." James might have been shocked to learn that, contrary to his prediction, careful English was not being spoiled from the bottom up but rather the other way round. Surely most of the bad language of today seems to come from what we are pleased to call the educated classes. Edward Shils has formulated this very point with precision. In the nineteenth and early twentieth century, according to Professor Shils, many additions to the American language "arose from striking experiences and they had a kind of sardonic humor about them, especially those which came from the lower classes, which seemed to bespeak the rugged experience which persons in those classes characteristically could not avoid. . . . Many of the unpleasant words of the present are manufactured not from experience but from doctrine."

No mystery about what these doctrines are: they are the doctrines of psychology and sociology, of military strategy and political science, of technology and literary and art criticism. Bad language is no longer picked up on the streets but in the classroom, where verbal gaseousness is part of the atmosphere. From the college classrooms it fans out into the media—and also filters down into grade and secondary schools—so that even if one is not able to go to college one still gets it all, through television and the press, by what is in effect a correspondence course.

A most interesting new book touching on all these issues, questions, and problems has the uncatchy title *6,000 Words: A Supplement to Webster's Third New International Dictionary*. Although available in a trade edition, *6,000 Words* is essentially the addenda section of *Webster's Third*, which first appeared in 1961, and it serves, in the words of its editors, two purposes: "to record as many as space will permit of the new words and meanings that have become established since *Webster's Third* was edited and to enter those older words that for various reasons had been passed over in earlier editing." But another purpose is served, that of a chronicle of what we in the United States have been thinking and doing over the past fifteen years.

Room enough can be found in these 6,000 entries for inspiration as well as despair. To make handy use of one of its own fresh entries, the book provides a "curate's egg" ("something with both good and bad parts or qualities") of evidence, which I shall get to presently. But first something needs to be said about the experience of reading *6,000 Words*. It is, I think, a book to read straight through, rather than to skip and skim around in. Going through its pages can best be likened to going through the pages of a snapshot album, but with this decisive difference: the feeling one comes away with is not nostalgia but something closer to its opposite, historical revulsion. "Car coat," "hot pants," "hipsterism," "hippiedom," "rap session," "sensitivity training," "teeny bopper"—those were the days, my friend, thank God they're at an end.

As a supplement to *Webster's Third*, *6,000 Words* continues the *Third's* permissive principles. That is to say, no standards are invoked for inclusion of a word, except that it show up with sufficient frequency in contemporary speech and writing. The definitions, as the editors note, "are based not on an editor's idea of what words ought to mean but rather on the meanings actually given to words by the speakers and writers of English who use them." I should prefer a more prescriptive dictionary, one that notes, where called for, that an entry is a "cant" word, to use the term Dr. Johnson used in his *Dictionary*. I prefer this not out of grundyism, but because I doubt if a language can long survive in

health under a policy of (to use another new entry from
6,000 Words) "open admissions." *6,000 Words*, then, is nearly
useless as a guide but excellent as a record. Like the period
it indirectly chronicles, it is itself a curate's egg.

A historian of the future, with only *6,000 Words* as evidence,
would deduce that over the recent past the most exciting
activity in American life has been in science, medicine, and
technology. "Science and technology," the editors of the volume note, "are probably the most prolific providers of new
words today." Judging from its bulk of new words, we have
been living in a most productive period for space exploration,
physics, mathematics, biology (especially genetics), and com-
puter engineering. The linguistic legacy is sometimes poetic—"damsel bug" is charming and the astronomers' "black
hole," which puts in an appearance between "Black English"
and "black comedy," has an unrelenting fascination. More
often, though, the language of science remains impenetrable
to the outsider: "cycasin," "BAL," and thirteen different
words beginning with the prefix "cryo" do not comfortably
roost in the memory.

Elsewhere this same historian will find ours to have been
a time of either enormous deceit or enormous wariness
about being deceived. "Credibility gap," "hype," "shuck,"
"rip off," "fink out," "co-opt," "cop-out," and "gazump"—
this last a British import, meaning to cheat or swindle—
came into prominence. Life had its "hassles" and its "non-
events." (It also had its "media events," a phrase that did
not make it into *6,000 Words*.) It will have seemed less a sexy
than a sex-ridden time, when such words as "gayola,"
"group grope," "erotology," "fellate" (a verb), "dyke," and
"hickey" were bruited about—a time when a need arose for
the word "hetero" and people gave one another the "bird."
The "funky" seemed "foxy" and the "flaky" frequently
"flipped." "Far out!" was a common exclamation, as people
"got it on," or, as the case may have been, "got it off."
"Hardhats" and "hardliners" never listened to "hard rock"

nor went into "head shops," although some "honkies" wore "hip huggers" and ate "hoagies." Linguistically, it was a good time for "underachievers."

What, to ask the Chernyshevskian question, is to be done? I recall reading some years ago about a small left-wing magazine that asked that question and answered it by saying, "Nothing, absolutely nothing," and then promptly folded. But a great language does not fold; instead it slowly rots. Does language affect life, or does it merely reflect it? Negro slang, for example, was once by far the most inventive in America, with, among other words, "vines" standing for clothes, "sky" for hat, till a man's wardrobe took on the delights of a landscape. But in recent years this same slang has grown snorting and sullen: "honky," "pig," "get off my case." Shoes, which often used to be called "kicks," are now more often called "stomps." The new slang is a reflection of anger, and also of taking advantage of the opportunity to express anger openly, but one wonders if it is not also an aid to anger.

In writing about language, in considering the state of the lingo, there is always a tendency to assume a prelapsarian time—a linguistic Eden where language was once clear and crisp and fitted exactly its function. Bad language has, of course, always been with us: language meant to obscure, to deceive, to defraud. Yet I have recently been reading books by and about John D. Rockefeller, once the most hated man in America, who, although he never went to college, wrote better prose than any political scientist I can name. Doubtless this had to do with the fact that Rockefeller sedulously read the Bible, and suffered neither lexical impoverishment nor the hunger for innovation that is now endemic and that calls for changing one's vocabulary, like one's tires, roughly every three years. Today one cannot tell industrialists from political scientists; they both talk and write like bureaucrats who studied sociology. Examples abound—and from every field.

The literary critic Tony Tanner, in the *Times Literary Supplement*, writes of the literary critic Edward Said: "... he clearly has a massively informed inwardness with a whole other culture." Edmund Wilson has remarked about "massive": "I have also written before of this stupid and oppressive word, which seems to have become since then even more common as a ready cliché that acts as a blackout on thinking." Daniel Patrick Moynihan, who enjoys language as has no other man in public life in this country for decades, must have missed reading Wilson on this point, for in his senatorial campaign he remarked that his opponent was "a man who consistently and massively and only says 'no' to the tradition of decent liberalism that New York State has always stood for."

Things are no better lower down. Mark Fidrych, the splendid pitcher of the Detroit Tigers, can scarcely get out a sentence without half a dozen "rights," "mans," "you knows," and "heys." When he does, what emerges is the following: "I never envisioned anything because that's looking in the future, right?" Next to Mark Fidrych, Dizzy Dean sounds like high table talk at Balliol, Casey Stengel like the Old Vic. Why does a man as intelligent as Julian Bond say, as he did not long ago in an interview, "There was no provision for citizen input"? (Has he been linguistically co-opted by IBM?) In the same publication, the magazine *Southern Exposure,* we learn that "Chip Hughes is the Research Director of the Institute for Southern Studies, currently focusing on occupational safety and health issues." (If he—or is it the Institute?—doesn't stop focusing, he, or it, will develop a squint.) Why does a literary critic write to congratulate me on an essay I have written by saying that the essay is "eminently sane"? (Does it mean that other things I have written have been only moderately, or possibly barely, sane?) Who invented the hideous phrase "pick your brain"? Was it the same person who thought up "whatshisface"? Can any student tell why he likes a book without using the words "relate to" or "identify with"? Is there ever a "breakthrough" that is not "unprecedented"? Whose coinages are "prolongevity" and "relaxaction"? Is he the same man who put "the quality of" into the phrase "quality of life programs"? Or is he the man who put the "out" into "check out"? (Must make a note to check it—out.) What does "off the wall" mean? Does "reductive" ever mean anything other than that one considers the person one is applying it to as less clever than oneself? When John Hawkes is described in the *New York Times Book Review* as "Feasibly America's Best Novelist," are we to assume that one of the journal's editors formerly worked for an insurance company? Where did people in the State and Defense departments acquire the odious phrases "nuts and bolts," "nitty-gritty," and "the goodies"? Which is the deader word: "thrust" or "impact"? Why does my own beloved alma mater, the University of Chicago, offer an award to someone judged "Communicator of the Year"? Has this award something to do with eradicating disease; if so, why give it to a communicator? Puzzling, all of it, very puzzling.

These questions may be taken as the rantings of a crank. Very well. Yet, if crank one must be, a language crank at this moment seems to me perhaps the least useless kind. For the only answer I can devise to the question of what is to be done about the state of language in America is to develop more cranks—a national posse of cranks. Limits to crankishness must be set, of course. "Laugh at a man's language," Herbert Agar once wrote, "and you have laughed at the man himself in the most inclusive sense." I, for one, cannot bring myself ever to correct anyone in private, but anyone who uses language publicly—a writer, politician, teacher, journalist—anyone who lives off language without caring about it seems to me fair game. Such people ought to be made to feel, wherever possible, the sting of criticism; or, as many of them might put it, their "success experience must every now and then be interrupted by a sound rejection phenomenon."

Looking for America

I not long ago read with great interest that a writer named Dan Wakefield has written a book about American television soap opera. In this book, according to an interview with the author that ran in *Publishers Weekly*, Mr. Wakefield tells about his own addiction to the "soaps" and takes them very seriously indeed. He likens their audiences to those that once followed the serialized novels of Dickens, Trollope, Harriet Beecher Stowe, and Henry James. "People who watch today's soap operas are enjoying some of the best storytelling of our time," Mr. Wakefield says, and then adds, "It impressed me that the soaps included, and dealt with, people's lives as I think they are." Agnes Nixon, the writer of one soap, a show called *All My Children*, Mr. Wakefield thinks to be the Charles Dickens of our day. Strenuous claims these.

Although I do not intend to test these claims either by watching the television soaps or by reading Mr. Wakefield's book on the subject, I was fascinated to learn that Mr. Wakefield had written such a book, for I remember him as a writer of very different interests. I remember him, specifically, as an *engagé* journalist, a man who wrote about life in Harlan County, Kentucky, about the lives of Puerto Ricans in New York, about the harsh days of drug addicts, about the turmoil over civil rights in the South. I remember him also as the author of a longish essay, in *Esquire*, about how John Dos Passos, in the cant phrase deriving from Stalinism, "sold out." Apparently Mr. Wakefield has come to think that other things are more important. To him the action in American life is now elsewhere, and in writing a book about American television soap opera he is in search of the way Americans live now—of no less than America itself. This is a large subject, the main subject, topic number one, and here comes Mr. Wakefield to say that the truth about it is to be found most any weekday afternoon at the turn of the on-off knob of one's television set.

What's going on, the way we live now, the search for our national character, the truth about America—all these various preoccupations might come under the rubric of the de Tocqueville Impulse. How strange—and strangely interesting—that the truest things written about us as a nation seem to have been written by foreigners. Along with Alexis de Tocqueville, the list of distinguished foreign interpreters of American life includes Lord Bryce, Johan Huizinga, and Gunnar Myrdal. More recently, Henry Fairlie, the British writer, has made a contribution with his book *The Spoiled Child of the Western World: The Miscarriage of the American Idea in Our Time*. But de Tocqueville, in *Democracy in America* (published in 1835), surpasses all subsequent efforts, and his work will probably remain unsurpassed. For writers on American subjects, nearly any American subject, *Democracy in America* is a one-man's Bartlett's *Familiar Quotations*. In the sociology or reportage of our day, a quote from de Tocqueville has come to carry something of the authority of Scripture in an earlier day. If one writes about America in any of its aspects, sooner or later one bumps into his monument of a work. Apart from the extraordinary powers of observation and subtlety of formulation that went into *Democracy in America*, the book has about it an uncanny comprehensiveness. Everything of importance about our nation seems to be there; anything that is not there does not seem important. True, in de Tocqueville's book some things have gone by the board, done in by time; notable among the casualties history has inflicted are his chapters on women in America. Yet *Democracy in America* remains the discursive equivalent of the Great American Novel, the *Moby-Dick* of our sociological literature, except that in it the hero (de Tocqueville) successfully lands the whale (America itself).

Harrison Salisbury, the Pulitzer Prize–winning journalist and latest of a long list of sufferers from the de Tocqueville Impulse, has recently returned from his search for America, the findings from which have been printed in the February 1976 number of *Esquire*. "Sufferer" may be more than a little imprecise applied to Mr. Salisbury, for he was sent out on his mission by the Xerox Corporation and paid very handsomely for his efforts. According to reports in the *New York Times*, Xerox paid Mr. Salisbury $40,000 for six months' work, along with $15,000 in expenses, in addition to framing his article with two full-page advertisements in that issue of *Esquire*. "The choice of subject," one of the ads announced, "was left entirely to Mr. Salisbury and his editors. Xerox exercised no editorial judgment over the content." A member of the craft myself, I am all for writers getting as much money as they can for their work; and, having read Mr. Salisbury's article, entitled "Travels Through America," I believe the Xerox Corporation did not in any way interfere with the writing of it. The project seems to be similar, as the Xerox Corporation claims, to that of a corporation sponsoring a television special. "Now," the Xerox ad in *Esquire* runs, "you are about to see a new kind of Xerox special—this one in print." The only thing in question is the quality of the show Harrison Salisbury puts on.

Xerox, an old joke has it, never came up with anything original, and it is sad to have to report that the joke has a true application to Mr. Salisbury's "Travels Through America." As Dan Wakefield turns his television dial to the after-noon soaps for his truth about America, Mr. Salisbury boards and debarks from jet airplanes for his. The problem is that Mr. Salisbury totes along such heavy luggage—of an ideological kind. He appears to be, for example, an admirer of China under Mao, where, he claims, the extended family has held together and where the notion of serving the people is still revered by leaders. He greatly admires a high school girl in Minnesota who "looks and acts like her heroine, Ber-nadette Devlin." Mr. Salisbury has what used to be called "a case" on youth. Older Negroes and youth are the only two groups accorded his unstinting admiration. Now in his early seventies, Mr. Salisbury appears to be afflicted with the dis-ease known as youthenescence: the belief among some of the aging that youth can do no wrong. Throughout his article the vocabulary of youth is regularly pressed into service. "We are trashing our people," he writes in connection with American treatment of the aged. People he visits are "deep into" Jung and ecology. Others are keeping a "low profile" or living their own "lifestyle." Things, for Mr. Salisbury, "all hang out." Such language is the verbal equivalent of denim, and is unseemly when worn by an older man.

Early in his article Mr. Salisbury writes: "Let me be hon-est. I cannot put it *all* together." But he is mistaken here. He has put it all together. Every current cliché about Amer-ica is to be found in his article. Aloft or aground, Mr. Salis-bury always has time to pay uncritical homage to every scrap of received opinion, every shred of conventional wis-dom mouthed or scribbled about the United States. We are a violent country. We are a country ruled by a matriarchy. Vietnam remains a festering wound in our stomach. Our cities are jungles. Our countryside is being eaten up. Youth of the seventies is not as passionate as youth of the sixties. Youth generally, though, is as dependably idealistic as taxi drivers encountered in Mr. Salisbury's pages are dependa-bly mean-spirited. Truths, half-truths, quarter-truths, tenth-

truths, outright falsehoods, all slosh together in this cliché
pudding of his devising. Visits Mr. Salisbury makes to Robert Bly, Hunter Thompson, Daniel Ellsberg, and Charles
Reich, all of whom he openly admires, are utterly predictable, his conversations with each man bearing the same
relationship to intellectual discourse as Muzak does to music: prepackaged, flat, heard too often. So sodden with
clichés is Mr. Salisbury's "Travels Through America" that
even when he describes a landscape one expects to be
shown a color-slide.

No, Harrison Salisbury is decidedly not the Alexis de
Tocqueville of our age. Insisting upon his optimism about
America throughout his article, he ends up with an unearned
quotation from the great French writer himself: "Future
events, whatever they may be, will not deprive the Americans
of their climate or their inland seas, their great rivers or their
exuberant soil. Nor will bad laws, revolutions and anarchy be
able to obliterate that love of prosperity and spirit of enterprise which seem to be the distinctive characteristic of their
race or extinguish altogether the knowledge that guides them
on their way." One finally puts down "Travels Through
America" thinking that, instead of Harrison Salisbury on
Alexis de Tocqueville, how much more interesting it would be
to have Alexis de Tocqueville on Harrison Salisbury.

What if de Tocqueville were to return to America today,
prepared to write a second and contemporary version of *Democracy in America?* Suppose, further, that he came to you,
armed with a letter of introduction, to ask advice on how
best he might proceed on his new researches. What advice
ought he to be given?

If de Tocqueville is to make a useful start in understanding, as he might put it, "the uncertain physiognomy" of our
country, I should suggest two indispensable items to him: an
American Express card and a copy of Evelyn Waugh's slender novel about modern journalism, *Scoop.* The first will

facilitate his getting round the country; the second, although written roughly forty years ago by an Englishman, will facilitate his understanding of the contemporary intellectual terrain over which he will be traveling. In *Democracy in America* de Tocqueville tended to scant the press, allowing it only scattered pages—most of them, to be sure, pure gold, as in the following: "To cull the inestimable benefits assured by freedom of the press, it is necessary to put up with the inevitable evils springing therefrom. The wish to enjoy the former and avoid the latter is to indulge in one of those illusions with which sick nations soothe themselves when, weary of struggle and exhausted by exertion, they seek means to allow hostile opinions and contradictory principles to exist together at the same time—in the same land." That is excellent, but one wonders if it doesn't come at things at rather too high a level of generality. An underpinning of sorts from Waugh might prove salutary, as in the following definition of the news by one of the characters in *Scoop*, himself a journalist: "News is what a chap who doesn't care much about anything wants to read. And it's only news until he's read it. After that it's dead."

De Tocqueville is famous for his perspicacity, his supreme intelligence, and wit, but the quality of his sense of humor is not so well known. If he is to write a book about contemporary America, his humor had better be of the first order. A sense of humor might well be required for the first exercise I would suggest for his new attempt to understand America. As a further introduction to our national life, after nearly a century and a half away from it, I think it would be useful for him to find out all he can about the following list of people:

1. Linda Ronstadt   6. Bob Guccione
2. Ed ("Too Tall") Jones 7. Werner Erhard
3. Halston   8. John Belushi
4. Bianca Jagger   9. Stevie Wonder
5. Waylon Jennings   10. Gore Vidal

This list may have the look of frivolity about it, but allow me to offer my assurance about both my earnestness and the thought that went into its compilation. First, anyone who does not know these names cannot be said to know contemporary America. Second, the list gives a fine sense of the circus quality of much of our national life. And, third, everyone on this list either earns large sums of money or garners a great deal of publicity—and in most instances both. Because wealth and fame are two of the traditional rewards societies pay to those they value most, it will be useful for de Tocqueville to know about some of the men and women contemporary America so rewards. To take account of the services they provide, to understand the reasons why they have been thrust (or in some cases been able to thrust themselves) into the limelight should prove enlightening to a man of de Tocqueville's extraordinary subtlety of observation. Besides, it would be a splendid thing in itself to have de Tocqueville, a master in the portrayal and understanding of such figures as Louis-Philippe, Lamartine, and Louis Napoleon, apply these same skills to Ed ("Too Tall") Jones, Waylon Jennings, and Gore Vidal. What, one wonders, would he make of men raised to national exaltation, one of whom has the job of knocking senseless other men called quarterbacks; another of whom writes and sings songs about truck drivers, unrequited love, and heavy drinking; and yet another of whom tells his countrymen, over and over again in essays and novels, what utter swine they are?

If de Tocqueville would wish, as he put it in his *Recollections*, "to consider the state of mores and opinions" in the United States, he would, alas, have to spend a good bit of his time investigating our media. These have come to have a vaster role than even the prophetic de Tocqueville could have imagined. What the media in America tell us sometimes seems all we know, but always considerably less than we need to know. Because the manifestations of the media are ubiquitous in contemporary America, the visiting Frenchman could doubtless use some help to discover which of them would most repay his attention.

First among them would have to be the *New York Times*, both daily and Sunday editions, which is the nearest thing we have to a national newspaper and which is, as it happens, my own favorite soap opera. I would instruct M. de Tocqueville to read that newspaper as I do, bypassing the editorials and lightly skimming the major news about politics and economics and international affairs, so as to reserve his concentration for its oddments. The "family/style" page, with its concern for status in matters of food, dress, and furniture, is certainly worthy of his serious attention. So, too, are those two- and three-inch fillers at the bottoms of columns about "Coup Attempt in Zaire" and "Arab-Israeli Border Clash." Gold is sometimes buried down there, such as the nugget I once discovered about a man who wished to be—and apparently was—buried in his new Lincoln Continental (whether sitting up at the wheel or stretched out along the back seat, an important detail, the story did not say). De Tocqueville might look as well at those stories that creep into the newspaper on slow news days ("Chief Justice Warren, on Eightieth Birthday, Sees No Trend in Berger Court" is one I shall always prize) and ponder what they are doing there. Surely he would find on his own, and find fascinating, the Op-Ed page, that splendid simulacrum of the notion of "dialogue," which, as construed by the *New York Times*, is an exercise in playing both ends without a middle.

In a letter of 1843 to Eugène Stoffels, de Tocqueville wrote: "Man with his vices, his weaknesses, his virtues, this confused medley of good and ill, high and low, goodness and depravity, is yet, take him all in all, the object on earth most worthy of study, of interest, of pity, of attachment, and of admiration. And since we haven't got angels, we can attach ourselves to nothing greater and more worthy of our devotion than our own kind." De Tocqueville would perhaps not be surprised to find his interest in man—that is, in people—mirrored in contemporary Americans, although he would doubtless have worthwhile things to say about the form this interest has taken in recent years in the media. It found its first outlet, this peculiar interest, in the "People" and "Newsmakers" sections of *Time* and *Newsweek*, whence it was picked up by the *New York Times* and nearly every other major American newspaper. These sections usually consist of gossip, short takes—sometimes of a few lines, sometimes of a middling-size paragraph—and are generally the most read segments of those magazines and newspapers in which they appear. So well read are they that, inevitably, Time-Life, Inc., has in recent years published a magazine exclusively catering to this interest. *People* it is called, but "Peephole" is how it is best thought of, and it ought to be commended to M. de Tocqueville's attention.

The editors at *People*, as Mr. Harrison Salisbury might say, let it all hang out or, more precisely, attempt to get everyone else to let theirs hang out. Subjects for *People* in any given week might include Alan Page, then defensive lineman of the Minnesota Vikings, in his bath with his wife; the actor Jack Nicholson's hair transplant; Princess Margaret's love affair ("tropical tryst with a youthful suitor"); the forthcoming marriage of Miss America; the sex life of a shot-putter ("Someday, says Brian Oldfield wistfully, he'll stash away enough money to pursue his true calling—poetry and philosophy"); Steve McQueen's new beard; the home life of the Italian tenor Luciano Pavarotti; the problems of the chief of our secret service in guarding presidential candidates; the daily life of a midwife in Laredo, Texas; zippy quotes from Jack Ford, Sonny Bono, Jeanne Moreau; and more, much more than one might think anyone could possibly want. But the appetite for such trivia is unslakable, as is, apparently, the appetite for celebrity. Here I should refer M. de Tocqueville to the wisdom of a character in *Scoop*, who remarks:

> But of course a journalist is welcome every-
> where.... As a rule there is one thing you can

count on in our job—popularity. There are plenty
of disadvantages I grant you, but you *are* liked and
respected. Ring people up any hour of the day or
night, butt into their houses uninvited, make them
answer a string of damn fool questions when they
want to do something else—they like it. Always a
smile, and the best of everything for the gentlemen
of the Press.

Along with a subscription to *People*, I am afraid that one
will have to be arranged for M. de Tocqueville to any publi-
cations of Mr. Clay Felker, who once owned *New York*, the
Village Voice, and *New West* and, after selling them, for a
time owned *Esquire*. As Hugh Hefner once was to pruri-
ence—I do not mean to imply reform, only the entry into
the field of serious competitors—so Clay Felker is to con-
sumption (not the disease but the consumer's art). Like no
one else in America at this time, Mr. Felker knows his
countrymen in their basest aspects: unquenchable in their
thirst for talk about sex, power, money, status, and goods. As
a young man Mr. Felker studied at the school of *Esquire*,
where he was a subeditor. His skill is that of window dressing, of putting the best possible face on the lowest possible
interests. Especially did he exhibit this in *New York*, the first
of the magazines under his control. Who has the best corned
beef sandwich in New York City? Which of its celebrity customers are no longer regulars at the restaurant Elaine's?
What are the salaries of the celebrated? Are upper-middle-
class women taking working-class lovers? All this was inter-
larded with pages and pages and pages about indoor plants
and furniture and food and wine, the lot overlaid with twin
myths—that modern-day New York is an adventure of great
fun and that each of us, the magazine's readers, has an income of roughly $150,000 a year.

Although M. de Tocqueville may raise an aristocratic eye-
brow at the details he confronts in the pages of *People* and
New York (he also should occasionally glimpse copies of
Vogue, Mother Jones, Rolling Stone, and *Women's Wear Daily*),

he would not, I suspect, be much surprised at the general tendency of the spectacle there played out. In chapter 17 of part 2 of volume 2 of *Democracy in America*, the chapter entitled "How the Aspect of Society in the United States Is at Once Agitated and Monotonous," he, perceptive as ever, notes: "[People in democracies] certainly are subject continually to great vicissitudes, but as the same successes and the same reverses are continually recurring, the name of the actors is all that changes, the play being always the same. American society appears animated because men and things are constantly changing; it is monotonous because all these changes are alike."

Shameful though it might seem to subject a first-class mind like de Tocqueville's to the drivel of so much journalism, one doesn't know quite where else to direct his attention. Once upon a time, and not so very long ago at that, one might have set out for him, as for any other intelligent foreign visitor, a course of the best novels in contemporary America. Having done so, one might have been assured that de Tocqueville would acquire from them the important truths about the way we live now. But, sad to report, American novelists, with only a few exceptions, have ceased to perform their once traditional function as historians of contemporary American life. The action for them is apparently elsewhere, and correspondingly (and some would say appropriately) their readers are no longer so interested in fiction. A single essay by Tom Wolfe tends to make a greater splash, a more insistent noise, than a longish novel by, say, John Updike. Ours is preeminently the age of journalism. Here conditions are not so very different from what de Tocqueville discovered them to be in the 1830s. "Only the journalists," he then wrote, "strike me as truly American. They certainly are not great writers, but they speak their country's language and they make themselves heard."

A certain amount of legwork would be in order for Alexis de Tocqueville's second visit. He ought to see the West that was not open to him upon his first visit: Los Angeles, Aspen,

Las Vegas. An interview with a Chicago alderman could scarcely fail to produce fascinating observations. A black slum, a wealthy suburb, a singles' bar, a skyscraper, a lunch at McDonald's—these, too, ought to be put on the itinerary. Time must be set aside for at least a two-hour tour of Bloomingdale's department store in New York, if only to check the validity of the observations de Tocqueville made in his chapter entitled "The Taste for Physical Comfort in America." In that chapter he noted:

> But when distinctions of rank are blurred and privileges abolished, when patrimonies are divided up and education and freedom spread, the poor conceive an eager desire to acquire comfort, and the rich think of the danger of losing it. A lot of middling fortunes are established. Their owners have enough physical enjoyments to get a taste for them, but not enough to content them. They never win them without effort or indulge in them without anxiety.

Perhaps, after all, only twenty minutes at Bloomingdale's will be necessary.

Our distinguished visitor ought also to log in a few hours in front of an American television set. I would recommend the *Today Show* and the *Tonight Show* and possibly a few items in between: Walter Cronkite portentously reading the evening news, a situation comedy, perhaps a pro football game. But *Today* and *Tonight* seem important for him to see: the former for the jumble of American life it provides, the latter for the strong whiff of show business fraudulence it provides. As American types, Jane Pauley and Johnny Carson figure to incite excellent commentary on de Tocqueville's part. Would he, one wonders, fall into addressing the latter as "Johnny"? It seems rather doubtful.

"But mostly U.S.A. is the speech of the people," wrote John Dos Passos at the outset of his grand trilogy. What of that speech—and what would de Tocqueville make of it in its contemporary aspect? He was hard on, but not incorrect about, our use of language during his visit here in 1831. He remarked, among other things, upon our abundance of abstract terms, noting that "they make expression quicker but conceptions less clear." Permit me, on behalf of my fellow Americans, to say, "Monsieur, you ain't heard nothing yet!" Attend Jimmy Connors, our premier tennis professional, speaking of his mother: "And now, you know, I listen to *mom*, but it's on a relationship basis, you know?" Attend Mrs. Anita Hoffman writing to her husband Abbie: "I more than anyone else know all you have to show off, but if life with you were to be always admiring your trip with none of my own, I don't think I could hack it." Attend a television listing for *The Adams Chronicles:* "Continuing adventures in the lifestyles of the founding fathers." Attend, finally, de Tocqueville: "I wonder if vagueness may not have a secret charm for talkers and writers in these lands. . . . Democratic citizens . . . will often have vacillating thoughts, and so language must be loose enough to leave them play."

It might be argued that I have done us as a nation and de Tocqueville as a writer a disservice by highlighting the freakish in my list of items he ought to read and view. Yet it is, I would counter in my defense, precisely the grand jumble and jangle and jumpiness of contemporary America that makes it at once so distinctive and so damnably hard to pin down. Despite the fact that we are now supplied with more information than at any time in our history—newspapers, magazines, television, public opinion polls, statistical reports, all-day radio news stations—a case can be made that we probably know less, or (what is much the same thing) can make less sense of what we know, than ever before. What do people in America think? How do they behave? Is what is true of opinion and behavior in New York City also true of opinion and behavior in Pine Bluff, Arkansas? Are Los Angeles, California, and Sterling, Illinois, except for the fact that they both happen to fall within our national boundaries, really part of the same nation? Can what Evelyn Waugh said in *Scoop* about his fictional country of Ishmaelia not also be said of the United States: "As there was no form of government common to the peoples thus segregated, nor tie of language, history, habit or belief, they were called a Republic"?

While writing this column, I asked a friend what advice he might offer Alexis de Tocqueville were he to return to America today. "I would tell him," he replied, in an answer that did not want for terseness, "go home." Yet de Tocqueville seems scarcely likely to have taken such advice. He did not wholly approve of us in the 1830s, and it is probable that he would not be any more approving now. Given a choice, his tendency was to prefer aristocracies, although of the kind cited by Ibsen—an aristocracy of "character and mind and will." But now that aristocracies are more obsolete than dueling, and democracies heavily outnumbered by oligarchies and simple despotisms, his sympathies might be somewhat altered—if not his method of inquiry, which, whatever his sympathies, was disinterested, measured, and wise. To him, most trenchant of students of societies, the panorama presented by the United States might well remain tempting, even in its modern muddle.

Among his many intellectual qualities, de Tocqueville had a special skill for recognizing and resolving contradictions. Surely no more fertile field for this skill is available than America. What would he make of our combined confidence and our taste for self-denigration, our decency and our brutality, our acquisitiveness and our guilt about our affluence, our liberality and our conservatism? What, above all, would he make of the fact that we devote more time and energy to national introspection than any other nation yet remain most in the dark about ourselves? Would he find a source of strength in our ignorance about ourselves? Unity in our division? A strain of uniformity in our variousness? Whatever he would find, whatever he would make of it all, it is difficult not to believe that, nearly a century and a half after his original visit, de Tocqueville would feel America still offers the most interesting show on earth.

Boutique America!

Now that the dust has settled, the counter-culture's chief contribution to American life becomes clear. The most important influence of that assemblage of 1960s youth and its camp followers was not on politics, or philosophy, or art, or social organization, but on retailing. Yes, retailing. The counter-culture came of age simultaneously with the consumer society, and what could be more fitting than that its participants should turn out to be shopkeepers—that the prefix "counter" should actually come to refer to the counter over which business is done? Fitting, too, that the generation whose chief literary work (a National Book Award winner) has been *The Whole Earth Catalog* should end up living not so much off the land as behind the cash register. The vaunted greening of America, it turns out, has come to little more than the cropping up of plant shops around the country. Candle shops, leather-goods shops, organic food shops, macramé shops, needlepoint shops, handcrafted jewelry and dress shops have brought the commune into the home, or, more precisely, the neighborhood. If one lives anywhere in any of the middle- to upper-middle-class neighborhoods in this country nowadays, one lives in Boutique America.

To live in Boutique America is to live in a state of permanent transitoriness, a tourist in one's own neighborhood. "Tourism," remarked Lincoln Steffens, "is a moral rest." Yet there is little restfulness about Boutique America. Quite the reverse. A feeling of jumpiness pervades, a sense that the shops that are here today will be gone tomorrow. Shops are the landscape of urban life, the trees and shrubs and flowers of city living. But a blight is now on the land: the blight of uniformity. Some judge the interest of a city by the number of blocks of entertaining window-shopping it provides. It is not a foolish measure. Today, walking the shopping districts of many American cities, one experiences a feeling of dislocation not unlike that of waking up in any Holiday Inn or Howard Johnson's Motor Lodge. Where am I—in Georgetown, Westport, Greenwich Village, or Ghirardelli Square? Essentially it doesn't matter. You are in Boutique America.

Boutique America is the new urban renewal. Old Town in Chicago, once a rather shabby working-class neighborhood, was taken up, and eventually over, by the young and the rising middle class during the early 1960s. Old houses were refurbished, new stores moved in, the place became something of a tourist attraction. On weekends, thousands padded up and down its sidewalks, glancing into the windows of head shops, of bars where first folk-singing, and later rock, was featured, of record and clothing and candle and poster shops. A new neighborhood came into bloom, but it was not to be a hardy perennial. Before the 1960s were out, Old Town, or at least its main drag, had become an adolescent Skid Row, populated by scrawny kids with dirty hair and drug-empty eyes and young blacks made belligerent by bad doctrine. Like an island reclaimed by the sea, the neighborhood slowly sank into its former shabbiness. In Chicago, meanwhile, the action moved farther north—more refurbishing, more new shops of the same kind—to a neighborhood rechristened New Town. New Town flourishes at the moment, but it is difficult not to believe that a Newer Town isn't in the offing.

Ironies aplenty are involved. Chief among them is that Boutique America set out to counter the creep of uniformity in American life. If Boutique America could be said to have an adversary, then that adversary was Franchise America: that horde of locusts represented by such franchised purveyors of goods and services as McDonald's, Howard Johnson's, Korvette's, Shakey's, and other national fast-food, discount, supermarket, and motel operations that have done so much in recent years to chew up the country- and city-side. Next to franchise bigness, the boutiques offered goods and services on a smaller human scale; next to cold impersonality, the warm personal touch; next to the mass-produced, the handcrafted; next to grossness and crassness, subtlety and delicacy. An anti-corporate, an anti-technological, an anti-bureaucratic impulse appears to be behind the boutique idea. One boutique owner thus sets out his hours in his shop window, which read: Most Afternoons, Some Evenings, Probably Saturday. These little shops clearly travel under the banner of art, of individuality, of the good life itself. Might William Morris have applauded? Or might he have gagged? More likely, confronted with the works of Franchise America and Boutique America, he would have announced a plague on both their condominiums.

Much of the art of the shops of Boutique America seems to have gone into their titles. Never before has such furious energy gone into the titlist's job. Where once might have stood the Howard Street Secondhand Clothing Store, the Nor-Shel Delicatessen (owned, of course, by Norman and Sheldon), or Slotkowski's Restaurant, now instead stand the Rag-Time Boutique, the Moveable Feast, and That Little Bohemian Restaurant. ("That" titles are very big in Boutique America—"That Paper Place," "That Plant Shop," "That Britches Joint" are but a few examples.) Heads and Tails is a boutique in my own neighborhood that sells cos-

metics and women's underwear (à la Frederick's of Holly-
wood). Barnum and Bagels is a recent delicatessen. But
perhaps the best all-round title—best at pointing up the
absurdity of the artistic impulse put to the service of retailing—is a small men's shop that carries the title Ciao Rudy
by Eugene Rondheim. A shop with a byline, as if it were
not a shop at all but a short story! Can boutiques with
lengthy epigraphs upon their windows, dedications on their
doors, be far behind?

Vulgarity, like bad news, travels fast. E. M. Forster, in his
biography of Goldsworthy Lowes Dickinson, remarks that
"He wanted a democracy where everyone will be an aristo-
crat." In contemporary America, where nearly everyone appears to be—in the preposition of our day—"into" art, are
we about to achieve a democracy where everyone will at
least be an artist? To pursue this matter of titling, why
should retailers enjoy a monopoly? What of the professions?
Can we look forward to dental offices entitled Put Your
Money Where Your Mouth Is, law offices entitled That Liti-
gious Place, churches entitled Pascal's Best Bet, funeral
homes entitled Oblivion Unlimited? Ours has always been a
country of the widest possibilities.

Whenever Igor Stravinsky, in his later years, was apprised
of some new development in modern art—multimedia, perhaps, or pop art—he would ask, "Who needs it?" It is a good
question, and a pertinent one to ask about various of our
new boutiques. Who needs all these new plant, candle,
leather-goods, needlepoint shops? Hard to say. Certainly
many of them, judging by the narrowness of their specialties—shops that sell kites, say, or soap, or wooden toys, or
coffee beans—seem to defy the law of supply and demand.
They are a refinement on our consumer society, the larger
part of which spends a great deal more time in consuming
products than in producing them. The refinement is that
these boutiques seem designed at least as much for the sake
of their owners as for their customers. They have upon them

the imprimatur of the "creative"—they smack of the inventive, they smell of the adorable, they stink of the cute. Who needs them? Their owners would appear to be the ones in need: a new middle-class nation of shopkeepers, *boutiquistes*, artists all. These boutiques can have as their only justification for being the fact that they are extensions of their owners' personalities, representations of their expressive side; this plus the hope of showing a sizable profit. How else understand them?—for trivia have never known such concentration and the *esthétique du schlock* has never been brought to a higher sheen than in Boutique America.

Viewed as a sociological phenomenon, the rise of Boutique America would appear to be connected with two factors: the end of large-scale emigration to America and the arrival into affluence of the middle class. Immigrants, in this century at least, have tended to supply the principal source of goods and services to the American public. Uneducated but earnest in the effort to get a leg up, the Greeks ran restaurants, the Jews went into retailing, the Italians sold produce and became florists, the Irish (along with being policemen) worked as waiters and owned neighborhood bars, the Germans did a bit of everything. The uprooted thus put down roots. We are now in the generations of their sons and grandsons and great-grandsons, for whom such work will no longer do. The truth is, for the industrious and the future-minded, our much-maligned American Dream has worked very efficiently. Owing to effort, encouragement, and sacrifice, the son of the Italian florist became a CPA, the son of the German butcher graduated from medical school, the Irish waiter's daughter went off to law school, and the son of the Jew who owned a dry cleaning shop became a professor. Who's left, then, to mind the store?

Why, the middle class itself—or that portion of it composed of reasonably educated and reasonably affluent people who have not somehow or other found a niche elsewhere. Among them are middle-class women conditioned to expect fulfillment (assuming, of course, such a thing exists) but insufficiently trained to acquire it through work; and youth, that transient class, too often educated beyond their competence and always headed elsewhere. In *Down and Out in Paris and London*, George Orwell, speaking from his angry socialist side, remarked that in anything resembling a good society certain jobs would simply be done away with. Waiting on tables was one such job; perhaps being a shopkeeper or a clerk would have been others for Orwell. He might have been right, even though he was writing about the hierarchically arranged societies of France and England in the thirties. In our own un-hierarchically arranged society, however, it may be the better part of wisdom to assume that every job done well is worth doing. Orwell was spared Boutique America, where the spirit of democracy has made a mockery of such jobs even while people continue to live off them.

George Woodcock, in *The Crystal Spirit*, tells a delightful anecdote about Orwell and restaurants. Despite his working-class sympathies, Orwell liked the best food. Whenever he struck a small bonanza—a sale to an American magazine, or a larger royalty check than he had expected—he would be off to an excellent London restaurant, there to set himself up to a first-class meal. As a balm to his working-class sympathies, however, before sitting down to table, Orwell would remove his suit coat, place it over the back of the chair, and polish off the meal, working-class style, in shirtsleeves. A nice instance, it has always seemed to me, of having it both ways.

I know a restaurant I should love to have taken George Orwell to for a bit of Boutique American dining, where I suspect that he would have kept his suit coat on. The restaurant is entitled Fritz That's It!, exclamation point and all. Orwell, upon entering, might have been good for a few exclamations of his own, for Fritz That's It! is what might be termed a multimedia restaurant very much in the temper of Boutique America. Music blares, posters of considerable grotesquerie festoon the walls, dark and dim prevail. Whether to bring Orwell for lunch or dinner is a perplexing question. At dinner he might enjoy the Donald Duck, or the Wells Fargo Escargo, or Giv 'Er Liver, or Cheap Stroganoff. At lunch, though, he might be tempted by Fishyssoise or Anti-Fatso Salad. Recalling in *The Road to Wigan Pier* something of Orwell's animus against vegetarians and fruit-juice drinkers, I would not dare to suggest the Vegetarian Omelette or one of a variety of Health Juices offered. I have a hunch that the atmosphere at Fritz That's It! might just put George in an austere mood, so perhaps I would have done best to suggest he order Sorry Fred . . . No Bread! ("½lb. of chopped steak broiled to your taste and topped w/ steamed vegetables and melted monterey jack cheese accompanied by sliced tomatoes vinaigrette. Absolutely no bread or potatoes . . . even if you beg! $2.30"). The menu prose might have put Orwell off even further—he was a purist about the English language—but what would he have made of the waitress? If she at all resembled the young woman who waited on me during my one appearance at the restaurant, she would arrive at our table to announce: "Hey, I'll be with you guys in a sec. They're all screwed up in the kitchen, haven't been able to get it together in there yet. But, here, check out these [menus], and I'll be right back to take your order."

Orwell can be mercifully spared a visit to Dr. Jazz, an ice-cream parlor of boutique inspiration. For one thing, when one lights up a cigarette in Dr. Jazz a loudly moaning siren goes off. Orwell was a heavy smoker, and, should he have chosen to light up, the siren might just have startled him into dropping his cigarette into his banana split. For another thing, like most Boutique America operations, Dr. Jazz features a heavy strain of nostalgia—ice-cream tables and chairs, nickelodeons, old-style pinball machines and skill games—yet its owners' nostalgia figures not to have been Orwell's. Or mine. For myself, the kind of nostalgia

Boutique America specializes in does nothing so much as rivet my attention to the Now. Besides, any nostalgic journeying into the past is brought up short with the arrival of the check: ice-cream sodas and sundaes at Dr. Jazz run from around $3.00. The generation that coined the term "rip off" is now busily coining the proceeds from rip offs of their own perpetration.

If anyone senses that this essay is written out of personal grievance, his instincts are near perfect. My own neighborhood is, alas, currently undergoing boutiquification. Such a nice dull neighborhood it is, too. Or rather *was*, till one day large signs were posted on neighborhood shop windows announcing, Paul Revere–like, "The Main Is Coming," "The Main Is Coming." The Main turns out to be a Boutique America shopping center on Main Street. I shall provide a tour of it presently, but first I shall attempt to get at what I so like about my neighborhood and what about it seems to me so worth saving.

What, really, is wanted from a neighborhood? Convenience, certainly; an absence of major aggravation, to be sure. But perhaps most of all, ideally, what is wanted is a comfortable background, a breathing space of intermission between the intensities of private life and the calculations of public life. In the neighborhood, relationships need not become entangled, behavior need not be triggered by motive. In the neighborhood—between the drama of the household and the battlefield of the career—the casual reigns, the quotidian dominates. In the neighborhood, life mercifully flows on.

Like the tides of the moon, the neighborhood in which I live has its own regular rhythms. In the early morning hours, there are the nattering of squirrels, the twittering of birds, the creaking of the newspaper delivery man's steel-wheeled cart. Things pick up around eight o'clock, as people set off for work. Showered and shined, ready for drama or dullness as the case may be, they step off to offices and shops. Yellow buses pull up to take children to day-care centers or nursery school, and in the summer to day camp. The majority of the kids go off to grade school three blocks away, or to the junior high school six blocks away, or to the high school a few miles distant. The neighborhood settles down. A young mother walks by with her infant in a pram. A truck from United Parcel stops for a delivery. A cat pads across a lawn. An elderly woman, a cane in one hand, a shopping bag in the other, trudges by. Near eleven, the postman is on the block. After three, school out, children take over the block: a boy bangs a tennis ball against a garage wall, two younger children chase a dog, bikes are everywhere. Around five-thirty, adults begin to return from downtown, some having stopped along the way for groceries or for dry cleaning. Dampened and rumpled after the day downtown and the subway ride home, they have roughly fourteen hours to give over to dinner, television, reading, lovemaking, and sleep, before starting out again. With the dark, a new quiet sets in. Teen-agers gather at the park or down at the lake; they leave behind them a clinging odor of pot or a few empty beer cans. The streets empty out, and only an occasional dog-walker appears after ten. Safe though the neighborhood generally is, this is still the 1970s, and even here paranoia is the better part of valor. The next day the same rhythm will begin again.

Weekends the rhythm changes. Saturday morning the street jumps with people on errands: much toting of laundry, dry cleaning, groceries. A more fervid energy is given over to the serious business of play. Couples glide by on bicycles. Tennis rackets are unscrewed from presses, unsheathed from covers. Camping equipment is loaded into trunks or onto car carriers. (In winter, skis replace camping equipment.) A slower, more dispersed traffic is on the street Sundays: people lug home their three or four pounds of *New York Times* or *Chicago Tribune*. In warm weather three couples living in an apartment building north of mine used to bring their breakfasts out to their building's small front lawn—in training for the more spacious life of the suburbs to which they have doubtless by now repaired.

A more than adequate supply of characters is about. A Negro cowboy roams these streets: a man who looks to be late into his sixties, he strolls about in sheepskin coat, a ten-gallon hat broken in at the brim, curly white sideburns, a bandana round his neck. An elderly woman, pale and frail, walks about wrapped up in an overly large blue rain-coat, black men's socks covering her thin legs, a babushka over her head tucked in snugly under the chin. Sitting on the small bench outside the neighborhood news kiosk is a man of glistening ebony color, with a slender head upon which are deployed features of an extraordinary delicacy and elegance. So handsome, so photogenic, so much the grist for a certain kind of art photography does he seem that more than once I have watched a stranger with a cam-era ask permission to photograph him. He invariably com-plies, smiling exuberantly, revealing several missing teeth. A woman a few buildings down my block feeds squirrels by hand at her high first-floor window. Five or six squirrels scale the wall to reach her ledge, and the tableau there presented makes it all too easy to imagine them taking over her apartment. A man in a beret, scraggly gray beard, and matching long hair lives around the corner; he wears all black in the winter, all white in the summer, and does I know not what for a living. Central Casting is to be con-gratulated for supplying these characters.

"Nice day, Mr. Steadman."

"Not if you've bet on the Cardinals it isn't, Mr. Epstein."

He is a neighborhood shopkeeper, runs a dry cleaning es-tablishment, a solitary man with a solitary vice: gambling on ball games. Unmarried, of middle age, neither an addict nor a fanatic, he is a man who, quite simply, enjoys his gambling. Across the street from Steadman's is the shop of Mr. William Richardson, shoe repair. (Will there be men in future generations who will do such jobs, or will shoes be made to be thrown out when the heels wear down or a hole is worn in the sole?) Mr. Richardson is a Negro, a man of perfect diction and high dignity. Adorning the wall of his shop is a commendatory plaque citing his efforts in behalf of the NAACP. Up the street is Wulf's, a Certified Grocery Store, now in its second generation of ownership. Mr. Wulf, Jr., in his middle forties, is quiet, competent, and roughly six feet six. He once played basketball for Michigan State: one imagines him not much of a scorer but very strong off the boards. Next door to Wulf's, at the corner, is Leo's Pharmacy. Leo's specialties are cameras, which sell pretty well, and flattery of his female customers, which doesn't always sell. "A beautiful day, now that you're here," he will say to one of them. Or "Where is that beautiful smile this morning?" A block away, on Main Street, used to be Joe's Laundromat. A furiously hard worker and an unshakably cheerful man, Joe carries a tattooed number on his forearm, memento of years in a Nazi concentration camp. When Boutique America came into the neighborhood, rents went up all around, and Joe chose to move. Into his place has since been inserted Sawdust, Inc., a shop that sells wooden toys and offers classes in woodcarving.

I do not want any wooden toys, I do not want any lessons in woodcarving, though I did like to have my laundry done at a reasonable price. Nor do I want to attend classes in "mixed media on canvas," which I note are to be offered up the street at The Tapestree, Inc. Nor, again, do I want classes in macramé, which will be held at the Chicago Bead Company, soon to open at The Main, the Boutique America shopping center (they, of course, would not use the word shopping center but prefer "mall").

As it turns out, The Main is actually the second Boutique America shopping center in the neighborhood, both of which have been developed by the same man. (A boutique developer? Who says there is no longer any place for the enterprising in America!) That the two are only a block away from each other and may cause some problems of mercantile redundancy seems not to bother anyone. The first has seven stall-like shops on two floors, with a restaurant above. "Description is revelation," Wallace Stevens says, so allow me merely to give the titles of these shops: Creative Yarns, Mostly Handmade, Sunny Side Up (which turns out to stock items also "mostly handmade"), The Mixed Bag, The Print Mint, All That Good Green Stuff, and Artesanias. The stores surrounding it on the same block are: Off the Hoof (leather goods), Stonerope (ceramics, macramé, stoneware, et cetera), The Smithern (custom carpentry, handcrafted jewelry), The Tapestree, Inc. (needlework, latchwork, Rya rug supplies), Mark Levin Woodworks (custom furniture, interiors, and woodenware), and Ye Rams (women's clothing).

The Main, a block away, very nearly duplicates these various "services," with a few of what in the mail-order business are called "add-ons." It contains Circe (classical allusions do not care who use them), a women's dress shop also selling handcrafted jewelry; The Green Grocer, another plant shop; Wood 'N' Things, more wooden toys; The Brown Bean, coffee, tea, herbs, and spices; Slipped Disc, records at no discount; My Favorite Soap Opera, soap, stuffed animals, and other debris; House of Teak, second-rate Scandinavian furniture; Neville Sargent Gallery, original paintings, prints, sculpture, and jewelry; Amazingrace, a coffeehouse and folk-singing and rock emporium; and—a brief bow in the direction of utility—The Main Currency Exchange. Still to come are Windy City Kite Works, kites and accessories; The Main Stitchery, one gathers more needlepoint, et cetera; The Chicago Bead Compay, mentioned above; and Revenir, a pastry café where continental coffee is to be sold. A short way down the block is It's Natural, which carries organic food and such; and down the block in the other direction still another leather shop and ID—The Idea Store, furniture and knick-knackery. In short, the works: as Zorba the Greek might say, the full catastrophe.

But what is the point of all this ranting? One might argue, simply, that it all comes down to a matter of "lifestyle." Boutique America is the going lifestyle, and it is too bad if it does not happen to be my lifestyle. To which I would rejoin: What if one isn't interested in lifestyle, but just in life, in the flow and weave of it and in its need for order and tranquility? Does Boutique America promise a better life, a new and more intelligent order of things? One wonders. The Main, interestingly enough, for all its ecological look, is currently undergoing zoning difficulties. Its developer, it seems, has failed to provide sufficient parking spaces, and some people in the neighborhood have lodged complaints. Interestingly, too, it has been brought out that the developer, an architect, is part of a development group. Another member of this group turns out to be president of the insurance company for which one of the sons of the late mayor of the City of Chicago works. Much talk is in the air about underassessed property taxes and deals of different kinds. It may be Boutique America, but it still sounds pretty much like business as usual.

Yet it is not quite business as usual. It figures to be jumpier. How long can, say, The Brown Bean last? Will the Windy City Kite Works weather the winter? How much handcrafted jewelry, wooden toys, plants, and needlepoint are needed? One looks for many failures and much turnover of owners—a state, in effect, of permanent transience. In the credits for the movies of the thirties and forties, a man used to be listed as responsible for "continuity." We could use the services of such a man in our lives. In daily life it is precisely continuity that seems in short supply, the sense that things fit together and flow smoothly. Boutique America does not promise to provide it; quite the reverse.

There is an old story about a man who goes back to his neighborhood after an absence of thirty-one years. He had left when drafted into the army in World War II, and afterward had settled on the West Coast. Predictably, upon returning to his neighborhood, he finds everything changed.

Where once a family-owned grocery store stood, there now stands a supermarket. Where once a small Greek restaurant stood, now stands a McDonald's. Where once stood Kogan Bros., Jewelers, now stands a Just Pants. But he does note one remnant from the old days, Koussitsky's Shoe Repair, and as he walks by the shop it flashes upon him that thirty-one years ago he left a pair of shoes with Koussitsky and never bothered to pick them up. Could they still be there? Why not, for the hell of it, find out?

Koussitsky still runs the shop. A bent old man thirty-one years ago, he is even more bent now. Our man says: "Excuse me, Mr. Koussitsky. I don't expect you to remember me, but I used to live in this neighborhood, and thirty-one years ago I left a pair of shoes with you for repair that I never picked up. I'm almost embarrassed to ask, but I wonder, do you still by any chance have them?"

Koussitsky looks up at him, squints, then says, "Tell me, vas dey black shoes?"

"Amazing," the man says, "I hadn't even thought about it till you mentioned it, but they were black."

"Tell me," says Koussitsky, "vere dey ving-tips?"

"Astonishing," the man says, "they were wing-tips indeed."

"If I'm not mistaken," says Koussitsky, "you vanted a half sole mid a rubber heel?"

"That is exactly what I wanted."

"And von ting more," says Koussitsky. "I believe you vanted taps on the toes. Is zat right?"

"Right on the button," says the man. "This is wonderful. Do you still have the shoes?"

Koussitsky looks up at him, squinting, and says, "Dey'll be ready Vendsday."

Sad to think that before too much longer in America that joke will be utterly incomprehensible.

Jokes and Their Relation to the Conscious

My title, of course, derives from Freud's famous work, *Jokes and Their Relation to the Unconscious.* In that work Freud put forth the notion that there are ultimately no jokes—and, as usual, he wasn't kidding. At bottom, he found, most jokes had as their purpose either hostility or exposure. But as Freud found it necessary, as Peter Gay has put it, "to be rational about irrationality," so in his book on jokes he turns out to be good-humored in his finally humorless task. *Jokes and Their Relation to the Unconscious,* in addition to being another piece of brilliant Freudian analysis, is also a compendium of quite good jokes, and from his selection of examples, it is apparent that Freud loved a joke. This should come as no great surprise. "The attitude of psychology," W. H. Auden once remarked, "should always be, 'Have you heard this one?'"

As a medical student Freud wrote a histological paper of some significance in which, to make sure of the firmness of his conclusions, he went to the trouble of dissecting four hundred eels. For his book on jokes, one suspects that he must have listened to more than four times that many jokes, though in the book itself he dissects, at a rough guess, only a hundred or so of them. Being Sigmund Freud, he is never obtuse—and if not everywhere persuasive, he is never less than fascinating. Only with one joke in the book does he, to my mind at least, go askew. This is the joke about Itzig in the army, which, as Freud recounts it, goes as follows:

> Itzig had been declared fit for service in the artillery. He was clearly an intelligent lad, but intractable and without any interest in the service. One of his superior officers, who was friendlily disposed to him, took him to one side and said to him: "Itzig, you're no use to us. I'll give you a piece of advice: buy yourself a cannon and make yourself independent!"

Freud believed that what this joke is about is that "the officer who gives Artilleryman Itzig this nonsensical advice is only making himself out stupid to show Itzig how stupidly he himself is behaving." I myself think the joke is really vaguely an anti-Semitic one about Jews performing best when in business for themselves. Another joke of the same type has to do with the Israeli private who is doing poorly in the army until his sergeant tells him he can win a weekend pass if he captures an Egyptian tank. Lo, three weeks in a row he brings in an Egyptian tank, and on each occasion wins his weekend pass. One of his fellow enlisted men, hotly curious, asks him how he does it. "Very simple," he says. "I go over to our motor pool and take out a tank. Then I drive out into the desert till I spot an Egyptian tank. At this point I hoist up a white flag. When the Egyptian tank driver comes within hearing range, I call out to him, 'Hey, friend, want to win a weekend pass?'"

Freud was chiefly interested in the underlying meaning of jokes—in, as his title announces, their relation to the unconscious—but I think that the relation of jokes to the *conscious* has an interest of its own. The above paragraph, for example, touches on a number of questions about jokes at the level of consciousness. Ethnic sensitivities abraded by jokes is but the most obvious. Would the Anti-Defamation League rather not have these two jokes told? ("Incidentally," Freud noted, "I do not know whether there are many other instances of a people making fun to such a degree of its own character [as do the Jews].") Then there is the question of jokes and taste. Ought one to be making Israeli-Arab jokes at a time when life in the Middle East is dire? Can it be that the better jokes are no laughing matter?

The world is divided on the question of the value of jokes: between those who adore them and those who, if not outright offended, are left cold by them. (The world, Robert Benchley said, is divided into two kinds of people—those who divide the world into two kinds of people and those who don't.) I happen to be among those who adore jokes. In saying this, I do not mean to say that I am a fine fellow, of that caste of special and superior beings: the good-humored. I used to think that a sense of humor was an absolute requisite for friendship; and while it is true that most of the people I count as friends enjoy laughter, so, alas, do many people who are frivolous, or cynical, or even vicious. Idi Amin, I understand, enjoyed a joke, too.

Having said that a taste for jokes is no sign of superiority, I am nonetheless not going to demonstrate my mental inferiority by setting about the thankless and absurd task of seriously defining a joke and then strenuously analyzing the nature of jokes. Jokes, like beauty, are too various to capture in any but a jerry-built definition. It is enough to say that there are short jokes and long jokes, sweet jokes and sour jokes, healthy and sick jokes, and jokes that spring from whimsy, anger, or sharp observation and sometimes from all of these in combination. But finally a joke is a joke, and the way to tell if it is any good or not is to notice, after you have heard it, whether you are smiling. If you are doing so out of more than politeness, it is a pleasant joke; if you are laughing, it is a good joke; if you are rocked with laughter, your eyes watering with laughter, it is, quite possibly, a blessed joke.

Max Beerbohm, whose work as an essayist and as a draughtsman has brought so much laughter, remarked that "only the emotion of love takes higher rank than that of laughter." He makes the interesting point that love has its origin in the physical and ends in the realm of the mental, while laughter has its origin in the mental and ends in the realm of the physical. Beerbohm claimed that he could make nothing of the lucubrations of William James or Henry Bergson on the subject of laughter. ("It distresses me," he wrote, "this failure to keep pace with the leaders of thought as they pass into oblivion.") He was content to accept laughter as a great gift. He felt—rather like Freud, though for different reasons—that "nine-tenths of the world's best laughter is laughter *at*, not *with*." He held that "laughter is a thing to be rated according to its own intensity."

Max Beerbohm also said that the man who has not laughed much in life is a failure, and that he himself would rather be a man to whom laughter has often been granted but who has died in a workhouse than another who has never laughed but may be buried in Westminster Abbey. I like that exceedingly, because, measured by this standard, my own life has already been a grand success. Laughter comes easily to me. Sometimes it comes too easily. I have been seized by attacks of giddy laughter in lecture halls, worn out by costly laughter in the act of courtship. Once, as a younger man, I was actually asked to leave a restaurant because my too uproarious laughter nearly resulted in upsetting a table. I seem, moreover, to be able to laugh at almost anything, exceptions being practical jokes and the comically intended descriptions of female actresses by the theater and movie critic John Simon. Well-done slapstick—for example, a man walking into a wall or one taking a pie in the face—can send me writhing to the floor. George Meredith said, "We know the degree of refinement in men by the matter they will laugh at, and the ring of the laugh." I laugh at Henny Youngman. So much, then, for my refinement.

I should prefer to die laughing and, on more than one occasion, thought I might. The best laughs, what Mel Brooks calls the dangerous laughs (implying the possibility of stroke or heart attack at the end of them), have invariably been private. The comic situation, the splendid off-the-cuff witticism, the unexpected fling of whimsy, the surgical puncturing of pretension, the predicament so bleak that it allows for no other response than laughter—these, which cannot be jerked from their context, make for the keenest laughter. Seldom do I laugh at the written word, although a few writers can bring me to this happy state: certain physical descriptions by Saul Bellow, patches of straight-faced dialogue by Evelyn Waugh, bizarre touches by S. J. Perelman, a mere phrase by H. L. Mencken (such as his reference, in one of his autobiographical volumes, to homosex as among "the non-Euclidian varieties of fornication"). Yet a book of jokes, of the kind that the late Bennett Cerf used to turn out, leaves me tighter lipped than a Calvinist at a porno film.

Jokes—formal, traditional jokes—are, or in my view ought to be, social acts. The best joke-tellers are those who have the patience to wait for conversation to come around to the point where the jokes in their repertoire have application. Take, for instance, the joke about Yankel Dombrovich, the forty-five-year-old bachelor from the village of Frampol, who is terrified of women:

> A match has been arranged for Yankel with a widow from a nearby village whose name is Miriam Schneider. Yankel is, dependably, terrified. His mother tells him not to worry. Women, she instructs her son, love to talk about three things: they love to talk about food, they love to talk about family, and if neither of these works they love to talk about philosophy.

Finally the day arrives upon which Yankel and Miriam are to be introduced. Miriam turns out to be 4' 6" and weigh well above two hundred pounds, and to be without apparent gifts for, or even inclination toward, conversation. Yankel thinks, Oh, this is horrible, what will I say to her? What was it Momma told me women like to talk about? Oh, yes, food.

"Miriam," he announces in a quavering voice, "let me ask you, Miriam, do you like noodles?"

"No," she replies in a bass voice drained of expressiveness, "I don't like noodles."

"Miriam," Yankel returns, remembering his mother's instructions that women also like to talk about family, "Miriam, do you have a brother?"

"No," she answers, "I don't got no brother."

Worse and worse, Yankel thinks. What is left to talk about? Oh, yes, philosophy. Momma says women like to talk about philosophy. "Miriam," Yankel lamely tries again, "let me ask you a final question: If you had a brother, would he like noodles?"

A more patient man than I would wait to tell such a joke until a discussion of modern philosophy arose. "Speaking of Wittgenstein," he might say, "do you know the story of Yankel Dombrovich?" But I am not that more patient man. So much did I like that joke when I first heard it that I told it, without aid of suave transition, to everyone I knew. But as I cannot await a suave transition to tell jokes, neither do I require any to have jokes told to me. In fact, I consider it a fine morning on which my telephone rings and a voice on the other end says, "Did you hear that the McCormick Company went to court to protest against the common metaphor for death being 'the Grim Reaper'?" No, I hadn't heard. "Yes, the McCormick Company has asked that henceforth death be known as 'the International Harvester.'"

My mornings are not interrupted in this way often enough. Even though I have a small band of four or five friends who share my love for a joke, and we report to each other regularly, not all that many new jokes seem to come into existence. Jokes may now, in fact, be in bad odor. I sense that nowadays people think there is something old-fashioned, square, out-of-it about them. My own generation, the one now in its forties, may possibly be the last to be interested in jokes, although perhaps here I am taking up the line of every generation as it grows into middle age. *Après nous, le déluge*, one thinks, when the generations behind one think *Après le déluge, nous*. Yet there can be no gainsaying that certain kinds of jokes have disappeared because their subject has disappeared. The old standby jokes about the traveling salesman and the farmer's daughter are a notable example. Here the conditions that once made the jokes tenable no longer exist. Less of the population is now on the farm, more salesmen probably now fly than drive, those who do drive usually are roaring along on freeways, and the old trust that once might have allowed a farmer to be at home to a salesman in distress is now gone.

Other kinds of jokes have disappeared because a social situation has arisen that makes them no longer funny. Mother-in-law jokes, for instance, have all but vanished. Why is the subject of mothers-in-law no longer funny? Because, I should guess, the assumptions under which such jokes once seemed funny can no longer be maintained. Although marriage has long been a subject for cynical jokes— "Married men make the worst husbands" is among the mildest—still, the old assumption behind most mother-in-law jokes was that marriage was really quite all right except during those periods when men had their mothers-in-law inflicted upon them. Now that the divorce rate is up, and the troubles of marriage go beyond having mothers-in-law on the premises, the joke is over.

In "The Place of Laughter in Tudor and Stuart England," the Neale Lecture in English History for 1976, Professor Keith Thomas, arguing for the importance of jokes to the historian, notes: "Jokes are a pointer to joking situations, areas of structural ambiguity in society itself; and their subject matter can be a revealing guide to past tensions and anxieties." By the same token, they can be a guide to current tensions and anxieties. Why, for example, are there currently no jokes about Negroes in America? The history of jokes about Negroes is a mini-history of the state of whites' thinking about Negroes over the past four or five decades. In my own lifetime the radio program *Amos 'n' Andy* wrung laughs out of every stereotyped attribute of the Negro, chief among which were dumbness, malapropisms, and irresponsibility. Then, when the civil rights movement of the early 1960s got under way, something called the "Mississippi joke" began to go the rounds.

> The U.S.S. *Mississippi*, a ship manned by white Mississippians, has but a single Negro aboard. One day the captain calls the first mate over to ask the whereabouts of the Negro.
> "About two days ago he died, sir, and we threw his body overboard."
> "Overboard?" asks the captain. "Are you sure he was dead?"
> "Well, we asked him if he was dead before we did it, sir. He said he wasn't—but you know how they lie."

A fast and interesting switch: the target of this joke is no longer Negro stereotypes but the brutality and stupidity of people who hold to these stereotypes. Yet nothing significant in the way of Negro jokes has come along since. A single Negro comedian of real power, Mr. Richard Pryor, has proved too dangerous to appear regularly on television, and his work has instead been more frequently shown in the movies, where it is much blunted. The subject of Negroes has become, in Francis Bacon's phrase, "privileged from jest." Why? As an amateur sociologist, I should say because there is today a great unease and anxiety about the subject of the black population in the United States, of which a large portion has risen in the accustomed way up into the middle class, but of which a sizable segment still seems hopelessly mired in lumpen status, and this is no joking matter.

Quite apart from explicitly political jokes of the kind Mort Sahl used to tell, most jokes have something of a political implication—political insofar as they appeal to conservative or radical temperaments. A joke can be judged conservative or radical if, in its implications, it tends to reinforce the arrangements of society as it stands, or if it protests against current arrangements. By this measure the late Lenny Bruce, so beloved of intellectuals in the 1960s, was assuredly a radical comedian, even though little of his material was explicitly political. A single conservative comedian is more difficult to point out, for the work of conservative comedy is done by discrete jokes. "When we laugh," Professor Thomas notes, "we betray our innermost assumptions." Virginia Woolf made the same point from a somewhat different angle when she said that one of the nice things about having settled morals—and, one might add, settled politics—is that at least one knows what to laugh at. Tell me whether you think a good joke can be made about the subject of free enterprise or of public welfare and I will tell you a good deal about what your politics are.

Are ethnic jokes essentially political? For the most part I suspect they are, and the majority of them tend to be of a conservative cast. Their origin is evidently in xenophobia. As early as the time of Tudor England, according to Professor Thomas, "there were jokes against foreigners, whose characters had already assumed familiar stereotypes: the French were lascivious, the Spaniards proud, the Italians revengeful, the Dutch mean and the Germans drunk." Not the least item of interest about ethnic jokes is that they often serve as an index to the social standing of a particular group, and in any country. Over British television, one can still hear Irish jokes such as this one:

Paddy goes to his physician to complain that in his marriage his sexual powers appear to be diminishing. The physician puts Paddy on a seafood diet, instructs him to run ten miles a day, and asks him to call in at the end of two weeks. After two weeks on this regimen, Paddy telephones to his physician.

"Well, Paddy," the physician asks, "has your sex life improved?"

"How would I know?" answers Paddy. "I'm a hundred and forty miles from home."

Sometimes ethnic jokes can be self-reflexive, and often these are among the most bitter. "A kike," said the Jewish banker and philanthropist Otto Kahn, "is what you call the Jewish gentleman who has just left the room." This is a superior joke coming from Jewish lips but not good at all if told by a non-Jew. Its target, certainly, is not the Jews, but their insecure place in the polite society of Otto Kahn's day. An ethnic joke told by a non-insider almost always has the curl of a sneer to it, at least in the view of the insider. "The slap in the face," said the French philosopher Alain, "is registered by the man who receives it, not the one who gives it."

One of the many ethnic jokes Freud tells in *Jokes and Their Relation to the Unconscious* is about two Galician Jews, one of whom asks the other, "Did you take a bath last week?" To which the other responds, "No, is one missing?" Today in the United States this joke would most likely be transformed into a Polish joke. In recent years the Poles have indisputably taken the brunt of ethnic humor in America.

A Pole finds a pig in the middle of the road. He brings it to his gas station attendant, whom he asks what he ought to do with the pig. The attendant tells him to take it to the local zoo, where they have a farm exhibit. Two weeks later, the Pole pulls back into the gas station. The attendant, noting the pig sitting on the front seat, says to the Pole, "I thought I told you to take that pig to the

zoo." "I did," answers the Pole, "and he enjoyed
it immensely. Today I'm taking him to the ball
game."

Thirty years ago that would not have been a Polish but a
"little moron" joke of the kind I learned in grade school. (Examples: Why did the little moron tiptoe past the medicine
chest? He didn't want to wake the sleeping pills. Why does it
take three little morons to replace a light bulb? One to hold
the bulb, the other two to turn the ladder. Et cetera.) Now
these are Polish jokes—these and, as anyone who has heard
his share knows, others that are much worse. Why the Poles?
Why so much contumely suddenly aimed at an ethnic group
whose history in this country has largely been one of upstand-
ingness and earnest aspiration? What seems to be the case is
that the Poles, unlike other once-besieged minority groups in
America, have no bank of social sympathy to draw upon.
People will tell Polish jokes that they would not dare tell
about the Negroes, or the Jews, or the Irish, or the Italians, or
Catholics. (Jokes about Catholics, too, have largely disappeared. Anti-Catholicism, as Richard Hofstadter once remarked, used to function as the pornography of Protestant-
ism; hence all those foul jokes about priests and nuns.) True,
it is traditional to make jokes about the lower classes, as it is
traditional for the lower classes to have their own jokes about
the upper classes. But the Poles of the United States and of
the Polish jokes are of the lower-middle and middle classes. Is
it, then, middle-class aspirations that are being attacked in
Polish jokes? Or is it instead, more simply, that no society can
carry on without having a target for attack and that the Poles,
by elimination, are at present it?

The best ethnic jokes, it seems to me, are those that use an
ethnic element not as a target but as a background: the
scenery for the joke, yet at the same time somehow more
than mere scenery.

In the village of Tsrampel, the merchant Reb
Goldman comes home early one afternoon to dis-

cover his wife being made love to on the couch in his parlor by his clerk Nathanson. Dazed, reeling with shock, he goes to his rabbi to report what he has just witnessed.

"Well," the rabbi responds, "your course is clear. You must divorce your wife."

"Divorce my wife, Rabbi?" says Reb Goldman. "Out of the question. I adore my wife."

"Then," says the rabbi, "you must fire your clerk."

"Fire Nathanson, Rabbi? Be serious. My business is up 40 percent over last year. And I owe it all to Nathanson, whom I consider indispensable."

"Very well," says the rabbi. "Go. In the meantime I shall consult the commentaries to find a solution. Return to my study a week hence."

A week later Reb Goldman is back in the rabbi's study, a beaming smile upon his face.

"Well," says the rabbi, "I see that you have decided to divorce your wife after all."

"On the contrary, Rabbi. My wife is a wonderful mother and has for twenty years been a good wife to me."

"Then you have decided to fire your clerk?"

"Never, Rabbi. Nathanson remains irreplaceable."

"So," says the rabbi, "then why are you smiling so contentedly?"

"Because, Rabbi, I sold the couch."

This joke is irreducibly Jewish. It would not work if it were set in a small Italian village with a shopkeeper going to his priest; it would not work set in Harlem. It is a sweet joke, lovely in many ways, although I think there are people who would take exception to it. Yet in it is to be found much of the pleasure that can be taken from ethnic jokes which are neither squalid nor vicious. The pleasure is in reacquainting ourselves with a piece of knowledge that, in the best schools, we are trained to disregard: the knowledge that there is something intractably distinct about every group, however we might wish to believe otherwise. *Et vive la distinction!*

I do not think the world, giving way to ethnic sensitivities,

would be better for the absence of ethnic jokes. Certainly
such jokes are not now in the ascendant. If there is a reigning kind of humor, I should say it is psychoanalytic. Psychoanalysis—"the talking cure," as it used to be called—was
once itself the subject of many jokes. (One woman to another: "My son has been to see a psychoanalyst, who tells him
that he has an Oedipus complex." The other woman: " Oedipus, schmoedipus, just so long as he loves his mother!")
Much of the humor of Woody Allen, surely the most admired
comedian of our day, especially among the young, is psychoanalytic and not only in subject matter ("I'm never again
going to a psychoanalytic conference," one Allen joke has it;
"all those guys do in the evenings is sit around drinking and
singing, 'I want a girl just like the girl that married dear old
Dad' ") but in style. The same can be said about the humor
of Philip Roth, which is at its source, as are the conflicts in
his novels, psychoanalytic. Both Allen and Roth are very
funny men, yet much of their humor, like psychoanalysis
itself, does not bear retelling. Although the comedy team of
Id & Superego—if I might so bill psychoanalytic humor—
has made possible many a hardy laugh, ultimately sex is the
fringe beyond which it cannot get. The pleasures that psychoanalytic humor gives seem of a different order than those
of conventional jokes.

What are the pleasures of conventional jokes? Granted, a
habitual joke-teller can make himself a terrible bore, and
certain vigorously filthy jokes can be, as Freud rightly said,
"acts of sexual aggression." The tension brought about by
the prospect of bad taste emerging in a joke-telling situation
is always present: "Did you hear the one about the two lesbi-
ans, the Turk, and the cocker spaniel?" The pleasures, however, do outweigh the risks. "A new joke," Freud wrote, "acts
almost like an event of universal interest; it is passed from
one person to another like the news of the latest victory."
Freud also wrote: "Joking activity should not, after all, be
described as pointless or aimless, since it has the unmistak-

able aim of evoking pleasure in its hearers.... [It is] an activity which aims at deriving pleasure from mental processes, whether intellectual or otherwise." Telling a joke is an authentic instance of how giving can be an even greater delight than receiving. How else explain that retelling the same joke to a fresh audience never becomes tiresome, although it generally is tiresome to hear the same joke retold?

When someone tells a good joke, something extraordinary can happen. Most people, I have discovered, rarely have a repertoire of more than two or three jokes. But one joke can ignite the memory of others perhaps long forgotten, and soon the cornucopia pours forth. Topical jokes—about politics, celebrities, events—fade away, meeting their just fate alongside the songs of Nineveh in oblivion. But the permanent jokes, those of universal point and interest, hang on, over the years and over the generations. Occasionally a joke will be improved by the listener's response to it. I recall once telling an economist of the Chicago School the old joke about the airplane in difficulty, whose captain, in order to land the plane safely, had to ask that passenger who was of least value to society to bail out without a parachute—at which point a disc jockey and a used-car salesman got up in the middle of the aisle and started fighting. "I would like that joke much better," said the economist, "if two sociologists got up in the middle of the aisle and started fighting."

But the great point about jokes is that they all have a point. Perhaps they are out of favor just now because the kind of pointed clarity they provide is not much valued; or, at any rate, so one assumes from its absence from so much contemporary literature, film, painting, and criticism. If an analogy is wanted, jokes may be likened to short stories of the traditional kind—not merely in their brevity but in the range of their possible effects. Jokes can be ironical, philosophical, bittersweet, satirical—anything, really, so long as they are also funny. To the connoisseur a well-told joke is a poem of sorts, having its own special rhythm. In my head, punch lines from jokes rattle around quite comfortably alongside lines of poetry, taking on a poetic status of their own. I close with a poem made up of punch lines—a joke addict's wasteland:

> Oy, was I thoisty!
> The Kuala tea of Mercey is never strained.
> You don't like my brother—eat the noodles.
> An hour later you're hungry for power.
> After lunch the captain wants to go water skiing.
> How much do you tip the whipper?
> Comfortable, I don't know; I make a nice living.
> Hit the ball and drag Irving.
> I'm crying because we lost India.
> Patience, jackass, patience.
> Is not hell for Khrushchev—is hell for Marilyn Monroe.
> And you'll keep singing it till you get it right.
> What do they know about fornication in Findley, Ohio?
> So what's this vulgar crap?
> Funny, you don't look Jewish.
> You're velcome.

The Opinionated Librarian

A bookish person, I live, naturally enough, surrounded by books. Bookcases are in my living room, in my hallways, in my dining room; in my bedroom stand five unmatched bookcases, not only jammed full but spilling over, with books and magazines lined up atop them. Books do furnish a room, as the saying goes, but at my place they bid fair to take over the joint. The mailman groans under the load of my purchases from Marboro, Blackwells, Strand, and various publishers. One morning I expect to wake up, walk into my bathroom, and find written in shaving cream on the mirror, in the style of the old maniac-killer movies, "Stop Me Before I Buy More Books." To prevent this happening, I made what for me is a radical decision: to trim down my personal library. Although I did not know it when I first set out to do this, I was engaged in a task of the most intimate literary criticism.

I recall a conversation I had some years ago with a man who has a reputation for living simply. He is an engineer by training, a photographer by interest, and, though not bookish, very intelligent about the books he does read. We talked about a book he had just read. I do not remember its title, but the book had recently come out, so he could only have read it in a cloth edition. He made it sound most interesting, and so I asked if he would let me have a look at it. "Oh," he said, "I am afraid that after finishing it I threw it in the garbage." Stunned does not begin to describe my reaction to this act. For days afterward I rolled it around in my head, trying to get it straight. He had bought a new book in a cloth edition, read it—actually rather liked it—and, when finished, slipped it into the garbage as if it were an empty wine bottle. Was the man a barbarian? Or merely sensibly efficient? Was I contemptuous of such an act? Or secretly envious?

Put aside those questions for a bit while I attempt to draw your tears. As a boy, I did not grow up in a bookish home. But through one of those accidents that go by the name of Fate, I caught the fever in college and soon became irrevocably bookish. When I read a book, I kept it, rather like a Boy Scout badge, to display achievement earned. An habitué of secondhand bookstores on Fourth Avenue and University Place in New York, I also bought a goodly number of books—desert-island specials, as I thought of them—that I hoped one day to get around to reading. In this way I compiled a library of, roughly, three or four hundred books. Nothing fancy, but a literary man's library containing the modernist writers, the great nineteenth-century Russian, French, and English novelists, Americans of the 1920s, some history, the standard philosophers—small, as personal collections of books go, but mine own.

Then I found myself having to make a move, at my own expense, across the country. Because I was a young married man with small children, economy measures were forced upon me. Moving books is expensive, so I decided to make the supreme sacrifice and sell my library. A man from the Argosy Bookstore on University Place was called in, and for the price of $135 he carried several loads in a laundry cart from my apartment to his station wagon. A pitiable sight I must have made—a child watching the Christmas tree being taken down on December 23. Of all the books I had acquired, I saved only six or seven thin volumes of Max Beerbohm's essays, Macaulay's four-volume *History of England* (which I have yet to read all the way through), and a luscious green cloth-covered Bodley Head edition of James Joyce's *Ulysses*.

The story has what I suppose is a happy ending. I now sit in an apartment with approximately twelve or thirteen hundred books around me. I have reacquired all my Edmund Wilson volumes, my magnificent Russians, my Americans, my Frenchmen and Englishmen, and added a great deal besides. The character of my library, though still chiefly literary, has changed somewhat to match my changing interests: more history, more autobiography and memoir, a bit more philosophy, less drama, and (a new item) many volumes on language and usage. It is a reader's library, though, more than a scholar's. There is little in it that cannot be found even in a mediocre university library or purchased in paperback. Often I find it useful to have these books on hand— when preparing a lecture or writing a piece—but not too often. Like a diamond stickpin, or a Phi Beta Kappa key, my personal library is not altogether functional.

Let me now go on to a bloodcurdling story, though one that can only curdle the blood of the bookish. I see fairly frequently a writer of international celebrity. He gets heavy mail, much of it of a bookish kind. Bound galleys and review copies flood into his home, propelled by the dreams of publishers and writers that he will read these books, be swept up by them to the point of championing them in a public way: by supplying a blurb or perhaps writing a review. An intellectual to the bone, he is a wide-ranging and voracious reader, but a man has his limits even if publishers, apparently, do not. On occasion he has asked me if I cared to have any of the books recently sent to him. I too have my limits, and once, when I chose not to take any from a small pile he offered, he picked up the pile, walked over to the incinerator in his kitchen, and dropped them down. I gulped. Book-

burning, for God's sake! He laughed, announcing, "I am the
Torquemada of the thirteenth floor." My immediate impulse
was to run down fourteen flights of stairs to the basement
and pull the books from the flames.

Obviously, I have not developed the degree of resistance of
my friend—who is a virtual black belt, a monk of the highest
contemplative order when it comes to discrimination in
such matters. I still cannot pass a secondhand bookstore
without going in. In England, I head straight for Charing
Cross Road—street of Foyles, of other used and new bookstores, of a store filled to the ceiling with sleek new Pen-
guins. I read all catalogs, browse in all bins.

Books, like money, tend to bring out the neurotic strain in
the bookish. Some while ago, I was interested to read in
Walter Laqueur's memoir of his friend George Leichtheim,
the political writer, that Leichtheim was, in his writing,
unable to quote from any book he did not own. Others will
not lay hand on a paperback. Still others will read only
books in British or foreign editions. I myself cannot bear to
read a book in which someone else has underlined passages.
I can read the books of V. S. Naipaul only in Penguin editions, those of Theodore Dreiser only in cloth.

But along with being a tale of tears and of terror, this is
also a tale of human reform—it has an element of uplift. In
this aspect of the tale, necessity turns out to be the mother
not only of invention but of virtue. A problem of space and
demand was involved. To retain the books now in my pos-
session—and I do not speak of backlogs of issues of magazines and journals—and to accommodate those that continue to stream in, would necessitate radical measures: move to
a larger place, remove some ample piece of furniture or major appliance to make room for more bookcases, sell a child.
The alternative, only slightly less painful, was clear: trim
down my library by a hundred or so books and possibly
more. But which books?

The job might have been a good bit easier if my library

contained a great many fifth-rate books—an ample collection of detective stories, say, or of science fiction. But nothing of the sort exists to make the job easier; rather than fifth-rate, I have a good many second- and third-rate books. All of them, alas, are serious books, many of them, as I survey them now, a bit too serious for my taste. A few are biblia abiblia, or books that are no books: coffee table items or misfired publisher's ideas. Many of them, too, are not books that I went out and purchased, but are books that over the years I have been asked to review or that I have acquired in order to fulfill one or another literary task. A personal library often represents a man's character or, if it consists largely of unread books, his aspirations. But my library, while doing both these things, also represents what others, chiefly editors, have thought of me. Only my tailor measures me correctly, said Dr. Johnson, who usually went about ill dressed.

Attrition might make a start in cutting back my library, and by attrition I mean not to bother calling in those volumes that I have lent to others. One such volume is the *Letters* of Lord Chesterfield, whose advice I am now probably too old to make much use of, and the friend who borrowed it several years ago has apparently not learned much from it either (see Lord Chesterfield on punctuality). Another volume out on loan is Edith Sitwell's *English Eccentrics;* because it is at the home of a friend who keeps more books in smaller quarters than I do, more likely than not the book is unfindable anyway. The two volumes of Malcolm Muggeridge's autobiography, *Chronicles of Wasted Time,* which I enjoyed greatly, have been lent to the Torquemada of the thirteenth floor. Have they by now, I wonder, met the flame? No matter. The author of *Chronicles of Wasted Time* would probably agree that I ought not to waste any more time on his books.

Trimming down a library in this way makes me wish I owned certain books I do not in fact own—if only for the delight of getting rid of them. The novels of Harrison Salisbury, if I owned them in the first place, would, I should imagine, be easily jettisoned. Books about show business, about politics in Latin America, about auto racing; books with titles that begin *The Death of . . .* or *The Politics of . . . ;* books on new forms of psychotherapy, on urban renewal, or arms control—shelves and shelves of these, if only I owned them, could go without a quiver of hesitation on my part.

But I am stalling. The problem is, I have come to have an unhealthy respect for books, and this is not lightly shaken off. Part of it is a respect for books generally, but an even greater part is for the books I have acquired. Walter Benjamin, in an essay entitled "Unpacking My Library" in his book *Illuminations,* a book I intend to retain in my library, notes with characteristic subtlety: "Every passion borders on the chaotic, but the collector's passion borders on the chaos of memories. More than that: the chance, the fate, that suffuse the past before my eyes are conspicuously present in the accustomed confusion of these books. For what else is this collection but a disorder to which habit has accommodated itself to such an extent that it can appear as order?" A book in one's own library is in a sense a brick in the building of one's being, carrying with it memories, a small block of one's personal intellectual history, associations unsortable in their profusion. Yet this building from time to time needs landscaping, tuckpointing, sandblasting.

Books on social problems seem good ones to begin chipping away. Social problems in America in recent years seem to be distinguished by two special qualities: they are perpetually changing and they are never solved. They do not really go away; instead people merely grow bored with them. Take an excellent book from my library, Robert Penn Warren's *Who Speaks for the Negro?* Most of those who deigned so to speak—the book was published in 1965—are by now dead, superannuated, or have lapsed into obscurity. The Negro, in most quarters, isn't any longer even called

Negro. Time has done the book in; turned a lively and passionate work into a historical document. My copy happens to be in paperback and hence does not take up much shelf space, so I shall keep it. Another paperback in the social problems realm that I shall relieve my shelves of is an item entitled *A Manual for Direct Action*, which appeared in the early 1960s and offered advice about staging sit-ins and other protest demonstrations. One small piece of its advice, I recall, was for a demonstrator to wear two or three pairs of underpants when sitting-in, so that if the police dragged him off at least his bottom would not get unduly scraped.

Children of Crisis, Robert Coles's three-volume work, will, I am afraid, have to go. A few years back, I read its more than 1,700 pages, most of them interviews, and I can remember almost nothing about them, except for an impoverished Appalachian woman's observation that, after losing one's first tooth, losing the rest of one's teeth comes much easier. (Why we remember what we remember from books is itself a splendid and mysterious subject.) Chances are great that I shall not return to Dr. Coles's three volumes, and they do take up a good deal of space. Out, then.

I should like to accomplish the task of trimming down my library with an even hand politically. Because Dr. Coles has come to have something of a leftish reputation, it would be well if I could match his departure from my shelves with that of a writer from the Right—to keep, so to say, a certain political balance. The books of William F. Buckley, Jr., are my choice. He may be further to the Right than Dr. Coles is to the Left but, more important than such political niceties, the seven or eight books of his that I own take up much more space. Besides, Mr. Buckley is better on television than in his books anyway, and should I ever grow hungry for him, he will be within easy reach.

Fiction is my next big cut, especially contemporary fiction of very recent years. Borges, Beckett, and Nabokov, though I do not adore their work, may stay. The work of their imitators, or workers in the same vineyards—Barthelme, Barth, Gass, and the rest—I have come to consider English department teaching aids, and no longer read them. They go. Along with them goes a category of fiction that might be termed Last Year's Novel of the Year—fiction of purported seriousness with high commercial possibilities. Among such works that I am able to weed from my shelves are *American Mischief* by Alan Lelchuk, *Julian* by Gore Vidal, *Something Happened* by Joseph Heller, E. L. Doctorow's *Ragtime*. Continuing on in the dispensable fiction category, the great *Gravity's Rainbow* question arises. I found myself unable to finish reading Mr. Pynchon's blockbuster novel. I read only enough to realize it was a book which one might write an essay or deliver a lecture upon, but surely not read. If I go to my grave without reading it, which I figure to do, this will not be my chief regret. (A reviewer in the *Times Literary Supplement* not long ago wistfully remarked that, for all the liveliness of American fiction, there were still moments when he yearned for the fiction of J. D. Salinger: "One [moment] might occur on reading page 235 of Pynchon's *Gravity's Rainbow* where the girl is defecating into the open mouth of Brigadier Pudding and you realize there are 500 pages still to go.") Still, it is harder to get rid of an unread than a read book. *Gravity's Rainbow*, then, will stay, the rationale for this decision being, "Best let sleeping dogs lie."

As I go through these books of mine, criteria emerge. One category marked for elimination is that of books I have read but do not expect ever to return to. Another category is books I have bought but have not yet got around to reading for the first time. How many unread books there are in my library I do not know. Usually these volumes represent failed aspirations. Consider some of their titles: a biography of Benjamin Jowett, another of Anatole France, *The Selected Writings of Sydney Smith* (introduction by W. H. Auden), *The Emergence of the Steppes: A History of Central Asia* by René Grousset, *Essays and Portraits in Anglo-Jewish History* by

Cecil Roth, *Manners and Morals in the Age of Optimism* by James Laver, Saint-Simon's *Historical Memoirs*, and a beautifully bound and handsomely boxed three-volume Bollingen edition of *The Muqaddimah* by Ibn Khaldûn. (This last is a work I first learned about from the writings of A. J. Liebling, who not only once made a pass at reviewing it but used regularly to quote and paraphrase Khaldûn, the fourteenth-century Arab scholar, in his own pieces on boxing, food, and the press. What books I now have of Liebling's, by the way, will stay, and I shouldn't mind acquiring more.) All these unread books, too, must be retained, if only to show that I have not yet given up all hope of self-betterment.

Retained as well will be all those books I have partially read, sometimes only dipped into. Justice Holmes, in a letter to Harold Laski, once said that he had a puritanical streak in matters of reading: he could not, till well into his seventies, begin a book, no matter how poor it proved, without finishing it. What Holmes was able to manage only in his seventies, I have been able to bring off in my forties. Among the partially read books in my library are William James's *Principles of Psychology*, Schopenhauer's *The World as Will and Representation*, Leslie Stephen's *English Thought in the Eighteenth Century*, Van Wyck Brooks's five-volume *Makers and Finders*, Richard F. Burton's *Personal Narrative of a Pilgrimage to Al-Medinah and Meccah*, and Steven Runciman's three-volume *A History of the Crusades*. But I seem able to put aside less monumental works as well. Sitting on my shelves with bookmarks still in them are E. M. Forster's *Goldsworthy Lowes Dickinson*, Evelyn Waugh's *Monsignor Ronald Knox*, Henry Mayhew's *London Underground*, and Elie Halévy's *A History of the English People in the 19th Century*. All these volumes will remain; I have hopes of completing them. (I plan a long life.)

The books of scholarly and intellectual and artistic friends must remain too, although their number grows larger as I grow older. Walter Benjamin notes that "Of all the ways of acquiring books, writing them oneself is regarded as the most praiseworthy method." Having friends who write them is next best. The Torquemada of the thirteenth floor, who is my secretly wished-for alter id in bibliographical matters, deals in a rougher justice here than I could ever hope to accomplish. In a secondhand bookstore, I once saw a book autographed for him by its author. I chuckled, then chilled. I have not the courage to do the same: I too much fear someone might do it to me. Also, I have always been touched by a story, told in P. P. Howe's *Life of William Hazlitt*, about Wordsworth's first visit to the home of Leigh Hunt, during which Hunt pointed out to Wordsworth a copy of the *Lyrical Ballads* on his shelf next to the works of Milton. Wordsworth, normally severe, is said to have melted.

I see that I make little progress. Time for a radical move, a slashing away to make space. With teeth gritted in determination, I remove the entire contents of a four-foot high bookcase holding years and years of back issues of *Commentary, Dissent,* the *TLS,* the *New York Review of Books, Hudson Review, Prose, Partisan Review, Encounter,* and *Modern Occasions.* I love—loved in the cases of those magazines that are now defunct—these magazines, have myself at one time or another contributed to most of them, but efficiency here subdues enthusiasm. Macaulay once commented that he felt that the life of any piece of intellectual journalism, his own included, was roughly six weeks. He was mistaken about his own, of course, but otherwise probably not too far off. The back issues of these magazines go—with love, but go they do.

The cleared space allows for rearranging shelves. Virtue not being sufficiently its own reward, I take time out for a bit of low-grade comic relief in the juxtaposing of books. Next to Christopher Lasch's *The Agony of the American Left* I insert Woody Allen's *Without Feathers;* next to Nietzsche's *My Sister and I,* Caffi's *A Critique of Violence;* next to Silone's *Bread and Wine,* Brillat-Savarin's *The Physiology of Taste;* next to Norman O. Brown's *Love's Body,* Santayana's *The*

Last Puritan; and, finally, between Susan Sontag's *Against Interpretation* and *Styles of Radical Will* I insert A. Alvarez's *Beyond All This Fiddle.*

Back to work. My next cut is a fine one—many fat volumes. These are the books of what might be termed the "agitational culture": works that appear on the scene, make a great flap (and much money), and then merely lie there. *The Kingdom and the Power* by Gay Talese is such a book, and the same author's *Honor Thy Father* is another. Out! David Halberstam's *The Best and the Brightest* is yet another. Out! If Gloria Steinem had written a book, or if I owned one by Andy Warhol, they would be gone in this batch as well. Philip Roth's *Our Gang,* which I do own, goes. I remember that Roth's *Our Gang* and Talese's *Honor Thy Father* were reviewed in the same week in the daily press, one reviewer saying of the first that as satire it was of the quality of Swift, and another reviewer saying of the second that it surpassed Balzac. I reported these findings to a friend, who commented: "We sleep tonight—criticism stands guard." I sleep tonight without these books in my room.

I am getting the hang of this task. Because I am now not quite so hard pressed for space, I begin to look ahead to eye further possible deletions from my library for next year. Books of movie criticism are prime candidates. The same goes for all novels that assume no serious linkage between cause and effect in the lives of their characters; most French literature written after 1950; autobiographies written by Americans who have not yet reached their fortieth birthday; literary criticism that does not take a healthy interest in literary history or in the biography of writers; philosophy that does not at least make the pretense of being written with its readers' personal salvation in mind; and all psycho-biographies of men and women who have been dead more than a century and hence whose backs never felt the couch. Books of this kind in my library, take warning: prepare to meet, if not thy maker, then thy recycler.

Some books, however, I find I cannot dispose of for sheerly sentimental reasons. Two sports novels for boys written by the late John R. Tunis, for example, which gave me so much pleasure so many years ago. I cannot imagine getting rid of the books of A. J. Liebling, who has always seemed to me the superior *New Yorker* writer—with a more interesting mind and a more fetching prose style than either James Thurber or E. B. White. Not all Edmund Wilson's books equally repay revisiting, but I find I cannot rid myself of any of them. He stays, *in toto*. All of H. L. Mencken's books stay.

Apart from books kept out of sentiment, further criteria for retaining those in my library now present themselves. First, all books I retain should be true. If they are not true, they should at least be well written. If they can be neither true nor well written, they should at a minimum be well made. With these criteria in force, one might think that a reasonably educated man could keep his library down to roughly five hundred books. A sensible number, but I am not sure I can actually do this with my own library. I ask myself, given my personal tastes, critical standards, prejudices, acquisitive habits, what is irreducible in my library as it now stands?

W. H. Auden—most of whose books I have and all of which I intend to keep—makes a distinction very much to the point here. "Critical Judgment and Personal Taste," he wrote, "are different kinds of evaluation which always overlap but seldom coincide." It is personal taste, for example, that makes me value Auden's work, both poetry and prose. It is the warmth of Auden that attracts me, the idiosyncrasies and commonsensicality of his mind. In selecting books that will stay in my library, personal taste probably has a larger place than does critical judgment, but that is what makes it a personal library.

Books that I find I cannot get rid of, that I hope to go down with, and that my children will have to dispose of afterward, are almost all those I have been able to lay hold of by and about Tolstoy, Henry James, Chekhov, and Joseph

Conrad. I have a similar enthusiasm for a less great writer who was a very great man: George Orwell. I will not release the French aphoristic writers, from La Rochefoucauld through La Bruyère to Alain, men who have come by their truths less through power of argument than through refinement of formulation. I do not love but I keep the books of the dark writers, chief among them Dostoevsky, Melville, and Kafka. Perhaps I suffer blind spots, but I do not make any conscious effort to collect the fiction of Mark Twain, D. H. Lawrence, or Virginia Woolf. Apart from E. M. Forster and Leonard Woolf, I prefer to read books about Bloomsbury than to read the Bloomsbury writers. I keep the books of F. Scott Fitzgerald, though I do not think they are very profitable reading for anyone over twenty-five years old. I have come to feel much the same about Ernest Hemingway. I read Norman Mailer, but am unable to reread him, and thus do not keep his books. I would, in fact—to put it in terms of marble-swapping on the playground—trade four Mailers for a single nonfiction V. S. Pritchett any day of the week. I do save the novels of Saul Bellow, who, though a novelist, is to me the foremost historian of contemporary American life. I cherish the books of Isaac Bashevis Singer for their Jewish spirit, those of Max Beerbohm for their exquisite wit, and those of William Hazlitt for what they have to teach about intellectual passion and English prose style. Of single works, I cannot let go of I. J. Singer's *The Brothers Ashkenazi*, Edward Dahlberg's *Because I Was Flesh*, Ford Madox Ford's *The Good Soldier*, and Alexander Herzen's *My Past and Thoughts*. Nor of de Tocqueville's *Democracy in America*, C. M. Bowra's *Memories*, and Dwight Macdonald's marvelous anthology, *Parodies*.

Looking over my books, I see that I keep a good deal of poetry around the house. Not all of it is of the first quality, though I find I can eliminate none of it—too much like putting a kitten on the doorstep in a snowstorm. Of the poetry I do have, I turn more often to Wallace Stevens and e. e. cummings than to Eliot or Frost or Yeats. (Another instance, I suspect, of personal taste winning out over critical judgment.) Among the next generation of poets, I turn more often to Randall Jarrell than to Robert Lowell, and (recently) to Philip Larkin more than to either.

Another shelf of books I cannot bring myself to purge are those written by dissidents within the Soviet Union: Pasternak's novel, books by Medeyev, Amalrik, and Sharkov, Nadezhda Mandelstam's two valuable volumes of memoirs, her husband Osip's poetry, all of Solzhenitsyn. These are books I do not so much love as find necessary. One such book I both find necessary and love is Andrei Sinyavsky's *A Voice from the Chorus*. (Excepting only Hannah Arendt's *The Origins of Totalitarianism* and Raul Hilberg's *The Destruction of the European Jews*, I do not save books about the Nazi era. Why I should keep the chronicles of one segment of barbarian history and not of another, I do not know.) I like to have these books around; they are a useful reminder.

I seem to have loaded up on Roman history in recent years, most of it in black-spined Penguin editions, which I read for what it has to convey about human nature played out on the grand scale. It stays in my library, as does the two-volume Hobbes translation of Thucydides. To be kept, too, are the books of the lucid and nontechnical philosophers: Hobbes, Hume, Mill, Bertrand Russell, and William James. I shall keep Santayana, whom I do not always understand but whom I appreciate for his serenity. I have the five volumes of Freud's *Collected Papers*, along with some of his separate studies and his *Letters*. Even though I do not believe in his general system ("Sublimation," writes Nadezhda Mandelstam, "what gloomy German brooding in his study ever thought of this one!"), I greatly admire his peripheral wisdom and his sense of mission. On the matter of great men, I have of late become a pushover for books by and about Dr. Johnson. John Wain's *Samuel Johnson*, one of my better recent acquisitions, stays.

In addition to all this are other standard and irreducible items: the English novelists and poets, Shakespeare (but no Shakespeare criticism), Cervantes, Gibbon, Pascal, Rousseau, Voltaire, Thomas Mann, Proust, Joyce, and a Gideon Bible stolen from a hotel room. Then there are the tools of the trade: *Webster's Dictionary*, the two-volume *Oxford English Dictionary*, an older edition of the *Britannica*, the Fowler and Follett books on usage, Mencken's *The American Language*, and a fine slender book by Sir Ernest Gowers entitled *The Complete Plain Words*. There must be other items I have missed enumerating. . . . But in all it is enough to keep a fellow off the streets for a good while.

Having cleaned out these shelves, and disposed of several of the superfluous books in my library, I feel a bit like Henry James, who, having shaved off his beard and prepared to enter upon his major phase, remarked that he felt "forty and clean and light." An illusory feeling for me, of course, not only because I am most distinctly not Henry James, but because the likelihood is great that in no time at all I shall load up the shelves again. The current week's *TLS* has nine previously unpublished drawings by Max Beerbohm; I have tried but I cannot throw that issue out. Looking over my library, I notice that I am two volumes short of having the complete *Collected Works of Walter Bagehot*. The novels of Evelyn Waugh have gotten away from me, too—all I have is his autobiography, the book on Ronald Knox, and a collection of travel writings. Neither do I have an Aristotle. I will take all the little Oxford's World's Classics volumes I can find. I am missing my copy of Robert Penn Warren's *All the King's Men*. I would like to have all the novels of Conrad in the uniform J. M. Dent edition. I should like to acquire all these books—and countless others. Is there no end to all this, short of death? Probably not.

But I am determined to institute a rule to keep the size of my library within bounds. It is a rule taken from Cyril Connolly's *Enemies of Promise* (I keep all the Connolly I can find). That book, it may be recalled, was written in 1938 "as a didactic enquiry into the problem of how to write a book which will last ten years." My adaptation of this rule is to pledge myself not to keep any book in my library that is unlikely to interest me ten years from now. As rules go, it is quite sound. One problem it does present, though, is that, strictly adhered to, it would not allow me to keep my own books and other scribblings. The efficient life is hard.

Marboro Country

Under my desk sits a box that arrived some months ago and remains unopened. It was preceded by a letter from my publisher announcing that a book I had written a few years back was to be remaindered and that I would receive an additional twelve copies before it was sent off to the remainder bookstores. The box contains those copies. I have no complaints about the fate of this book; suffice it to say that it came a long way from realizing the commercial fantasies I harbored for it, which were not slight. The book had an original printing of 10,000 copies. When this was sold out, a second, smaller edition of 2,500 was printed. The book went into a paperback edition, for which I received, by today's standards, a modest sum. It was also brought out in England. The second American cloth edition did not sell out, and it has been sent off, like cattle to the slaughter, to the remainder houses, or what I have come to think of as Marboro Country, after the nation's largest single remainder bookstore.

Sitting there under my desk, the box provokes questions about publishing in America. One of these questions is age-old: whether publishing is a business or an occupation for gentlemen. At various times various answers have been given. At present, I should say, the proper answer is that publishing is neither a business nor an occupation for gentlemen. Today, by and large, a publishing house comes closer to being a combination of a stock brokerage and an advertising agency, but it is suffused with an aura of romance and craziness that makes it less competent than either. But then I am that raging and raving beast, an author, and, as anyone who has read even a modicum of literary history knows, the relationship between authors and publishers over the centuries has often tended to be, to put it gently, that between adversaries.

When my book was published I had resolved not to go on television to attempt to sell it. My reasons were not complicated. I wrote the book, I felt, let my publishers sell it. Moreover, after watching a good many authors put through their paces on television, I had come to think that their performances were supremely boring. Charming devil though I am, I had no good reason to believe I could escape the general fate of all authors on television: putting their countrymen to sleep. The year my book appeared, publishers believed absolutely that television was the best medium for selling a book. (Publishers seem to believe in a thing absolutely for roughly two years; then, just as absolutely, they decide not to believe in it.) My publisher pleaded with me to reconsider my decision not to go on television with my book. I called my literary agent, whose counsel in such matters I respect. A phlegmatic Frenchman with majestic common sense, he said: "I am afraid that you must go along with them. If you do not, they will say, 'Ah, intransigent author! The devil with him.'" Hoist by my own modest greed—I tell you frankly, I should not have minded in the least if my book had earned me a few hundreds of thousands of dollars, say seven or eight—I called my publisher back to say that I had changed my mind and would indeed go on television to promote the book.

The first stop on my tour was High Point, North Carolina, where I had been booked to appear on a morning talk show called *Southern Exposure*. My publisher's publicity department assured me that the show is watched throughout the South. A dirty mind is a perpetual feast, says La Rochefoucauld, and *Southern Exposure* called to my mind the image of a man whose trousers had fallen, revealing his backside. Although I had appeared on television before, I feared that in this instance the revealed backside might be my own. The host of the show was cordial enough, a large man got up in a safari outfit and high-heeled boots, whose good looks seemed to be centered in his teeth. After speaking with me about the format of the show, he brought me into a conference room to meet the other "guests" of the day. These turned out to be a married couple who were midgets and a Mrs. Westmoreland, not the general's wife but a woman who had won $3,400 on two different national television game shows. ("If you show a lot of enthusiasm," she later said, "your chances of being picked as a contestant are enormously improved.") The midget couple were to go on first, I second, and the professional contestant third; then we would all join together in a final segment to display our utter absence of common interests. My own performance, as I macheted my way through the perplexities, paradoxes, and dolorosities of my book, took only half an hour, although it seemed to last a fortnight. All through the South I imagined men and women watching me over their breakfasts, their heads nestling gently, asleep, in plates of scrambled eggs and cereal bowls.

Well, that was certainly hell, I thought as I left the television studio, but hell gone through for a very good cause—my own potential enrichment. I had some time before my plane departed, so I walked the quiet morning streets of High Point. Was there, I inquired at a drugstore, a bookstore in town? There was indeed, quite a large one, I was told, a block up the street. Would my book be in the window, I wondered, given that I had only this morning had my southern exposure? Alas, it was not. Nor was it on the current selections table. Three white-haired ladies ran the ample and commodious shop. I announced my name, the fact that I had only now returned from doing a television show, and asked, in the cause of marketing science, if they had my book or any requests for it. "That name again, sir?" one of the ladies asked. Clever readers will anticipate that no books had been sent, even though the author had been—at a distance of roughly a thousand miles and the expense of roughly three hundred dollars. That was when I had my first hint that publishing in America was not quite a business.

As for publishing being an occupation for gentlemen, that, in the modern era, seems to have been its early history. In England there were men like William Chatto and Henry Faber, the latter the publisher (and, for a patch, the employer) of T. S. Eliot. In America there were men like Charles Scribner and Alfred Knopf. Knopf especially seemed to epitomize the gentlemanly aspects of publishing at its best. The books turned out under his Borzoi imprint were notable for being handsomely made: elegantly designed, finely printed, solidly stitched. In literary matters Knopf and his first wife, Blanche, were connoisseurs; between them they put together a splendid list of American authors and an unrivaled list of European authors. In the 1920s it was Alfred Knopf who put up the capital for H. L. Mencken's lively magazine, *The American Mercury*.

If Alfred Knopf represented the best among publishers in America in this century, among editors at publishing houses the reigning figure was indisputably Maxwell Perkins of the firm of Charles Scribner's Sons. Every profession has its ideal figure, its exemplar. In law such a figure was Clarence Darrow; in medicine it was no particular person but the ideal of the tireless country doctor; and among publishers' editors it has long been Maxwell Perkins. At Scribner's, Perkins (who had been Van Wyck Brooks's roommate at Harvard) was editor for, among other writers, F. Scott Fitzgerald, Ernest Hemingway, and Thomas Wolfe. As his letters and the recent biography by A. Scott Berg reveal, he had all the requisites of his craft: talent, taste, and consummate tact. To his authors he was simultaneously friend, bursar, consultant, and (in the case of Thomas Wolfe, whose baggy monster novels would have been unthinkable without his editorial aid) co-producer.

I myself, during a stint of roughly a year as a publisher's editor, had frequent occasion to think of Alfred Knopf and Maxwell Perkins. The firm I worked for, like so many other publishers in recent years, had just been bought by a larger corporation. The larger corporation's chief representative— in effect, our publisher—was a man trained in accounting, though a type of wheeler-dealer not often found among ac- countants. To help pay for its academic titles, the firm pub- lished a series of books on boating. The larger corporation also had very recently purchased a golf magazine. At an editorial meeting, the new publisher, who did not pretend to be interested in literature or scholarship, suggested that we place an ad for our boating books in the golf magazine. "I know these jokers," he said. "If they golf, they sail."

I thought of Maxwell Perkins and of the British tradition of gentlemanly publishing on the day an editor from an old English publishing firm of distinguished imprint walked into my office. In a crisp Oxbridge accent he announced that he was here on a selling trip, attempting to sell the American rights to a number of his firm's titles. From his briefcase he extracted page after page, each one listing a title for sale, a brief description of its content, a biographi- cal note on the author, and a suggested price. I needed to concentrate, at various points, to recall that we were talk- ing about books and not something else: costume jewelry, say, or cutlery. By the time he had arrived at my office, his better items had already been sold off, and the remaining ones—treatises on land reform in Wales, social scientific studies even more dismally specialized than those produced in the United States—were of no possible interest. We chatted pleasantly until, undefeated and indefatigable, he departed to make his next call. After he left I thought of the old joke about the man in the circus whose job is to clean up after the elephants. When asked by a friend why he doesn't quit so undignified a job, the man replies, "What! And leave show business!"

Publishing, if not quite show business, does have something glamorous adhering to it—at least when viewed from the outside. Publishers purvey culture, the sacred thing itself, and so publishing is drenched in romance. One of the marks of a romance industry—journalism, publishing, sports—is that it can get away with paying small salaries in its lower echelons, for the reason that so many people are lined up outside waiting to get in. Further evidence that publishing is viewed as essentially romantic is its treatment in popular culture. I shall never forget a scene from *The Best of Everything*, a movie notable for its rich sappiness, about three young women who arrive in New York fresh out of college to make their careers. One of them (played by the young Hope Lange) takes a job as a lowly secretary in a publishing company. After months of clerical drudgery, her boss (played by the late Joan Crawford) gives her a manuscript to read and report on after regular working hours. Shot of Miss Lange pulling chair up to desk in front of sleek new typewriter. Pan in close to memo paper in typewriter, and capture the following words being typed out: "This novel shows careful delineation of character. . . ." Dissolve and cut to senior editor's office, which Miss Lange now occupies as the result of her good taste and trenchant criticism. Ah, the movies!

To return to what is called real life, publishing is indubitably an important part of culture. Even more indubitably, though, it is a business. The combination of business and culture is a subject fit for Evelyn Waugh, for whenever the two get together one can generally count on plenty of laughs to be had all round. (One thinks here, among scores of possible examples, of the salesmen for the *Great Books of the Western World* having to be trained to pronounce the names of the authors: Dos-toy-ev-sky.) The question is, at whose expense are these laughs being registered? Business is concerned with profit; culture is concerned with standards and taste. Although one likes to think that the two can coalesce in purpose, more often they are at cross-purposes. In any standoff competition, culture goes down nearly every time. The wonder is not *why* more good books aren't published, but *how* so many good books are published.

Perhaps the chief reason is that culture is often good business. In contemporary America there is a great hunger for learning, for art, for all that travels under the banner of Culture with a capital C. How else explain those endless lines at the King Tut exhibit as it traveled around the country, those crowds at art museums and concerts, the success of book clubs, the elevation to celebrity status of writers and painters and musicians, real and fraudulent alike? The appetite for culture is palpably there; at issue is the quality of the diet it is being fed.

As cultural caterers, how good are publishers at their jobs? Well, today they look increasingly as if they were in the fast-food business—so insubstantial and mass produced do their products sometimes seem. "Nowadays everything grows old in a few hours; reputation fades, a work passes away in a moment. Everybody writes; nobody reads seriously." That remark, which appears to have a precise application to our own day, was actually uttered by Chateaubriand in 1836. Yet over the years remarks of this tenor have been made with greater intensity and more careful elaboration. In his essay "Civilization," for example, John Stuart Mill wrote:

> The world reads too much and too quickly to read well. When books were few, to get through one was a work of time and labour: what was written

with thought was read with thought, and with a
desire to extract from it as much of the materials
of knowledge as possible. But when almost every
person who can spell, can and will write, what is
to be done? . . . The world, in consequence, gorges
itself with intellectual food, and in order to swallow the more, *bolts* it.

Closer to our time, Albert Jay Nock, in his *Memoirs of a
Superfluous Man,* comments on the rich literary fare of his
youth in the 1880s and connects the demise of high-quality
publishing with the rising literacy of the American public.
The "reason why good literature was more easily accessible
then than now," Nock wrote, "is that the portion of literacy
in our population was much lower, and publishers were not
under such heavy economic pressure to block up the access
to good literature with trash." Nock was not interested in
turning back to a largely illiterate society, but he was concerned to show the effects of what one might term the exten-
sion of the reading franchise to ever greater numbers.
Despite the enormous growth both in literacy and in population over the period from his boyhood to his late maturity,
Nock noted that the circulation of *Harper's* magazine was
fully a third larger at a time when the country was only half
as populous. Other periodicals, too, published thicker issues
of a better quality in their earlier years. What brought this
about? *Mutatis mutandis,* Nock saw Gresham's law at work
in publishing. While the increase in literacy and population
brought a widened readership for books, Nock held, along
with Mill, that there was no reason to believe it was of necessity a better readership. But the widened audience did
mean a widened potential market, and hence a much increased potential for larger profits. Yet, as Nock saw it, there
were grave problems.

This market was unsteady; being based on nothing but irrational fancy, it had its ups and downs,
its hot and cold fits of susceptibility or indiffer-

ence towards this-or-that type of produce, this-or-
that lure of sensational appeal. Forecasting such a
market became mostly guesswork, and the character of publishing changed considerably in consequence; from a business it became essentially a
gamble bolstered by shrewdness in a meretricious
mode of salesmanship. Thus the operation of
Gresham's law progressively edged publishers farther and farther out of the category of merchants,
properly so called, and farther towards the category of gamblers and touts.

Gamblers and touts. Exactly. Except that most publishers
tout themselves, talking themselves into what they hope will
be commercial winners. ("I know these jokers. If they golf,
they sail.") Thus publishers bet on their hunches—and these,
like everyone else's hunches, are at least as often wrong as
right. One year technology is projected to be the hot subject,
so a plethora of books about it are published. Then the
hunch is movies, so books about movies come rolling off the
presses. Suddenly publishers decide that ecology is where
the action is. Yet the action doesn't remain there for long; it
switches to books about the condition of women. Jews read
more than any other single group—such are the subtle findings of publishing research into the market—so a glut of
books of varying quality aimed, as they say, at "hitting the
Jewish market" are churned out. Also to be regularly "hit" is
the fabled youth market—"fabled" because no one has ever
been able to prove that a youth market for books exists.
Then ethnicity becomes topic number one. Touting becomes
infectious, spreading from publishers to authors and an-
thologists. From my days as a publisher's editor, I prize a
letter from a long-shot artist who wrote to me offering to put
together for our firm the following four anthologies: *Growing
Up Black, Growing Up Jewish, Growing Up Puerto Rican*, and
Growing Up Gay.

In the same spirit, I prize the listings of Marboro's sales of
remaindered books. These listings can be likened to the

green sheet of tips sold at the racetrack, except that the
Marboro listing is for the most part composed of losers,
bright publishing ideas that never came off. Reading over
the titles, one wonders how anyone was ever able to hypno-
tize himself into the belief that a market for such books
could possibly exist. There is an old publishing joke that the
best possible title for a best seller in America would be *Lincoln's Doctor's Dog* and the worst title would be *Canada:
Sleeping Giant to the North.* But the following titles, taken
from a recent Marboro mailing, are no joke; these dogs
really do exist: *Skewer Cooking Around the World; The Peter
Principle Calendar; Gene Kelly; Moonstruck: An Anthology of
Lunar Poetry; Bitching; Car Badges of the World; Robot: The
Mechanical Monster and the Movies; Erotic Fantasies; Cre-
ative Crepe Cooking; The Cinema of Dirk Bogarde; The Bar
Mitzvah Book; The Photography of Rock; Parents' Guide to
Allergy in Children; 52 Weeks to a Great New Life; The Other
Half of the Egg; Instant Menu Translators; Anyone Can Still
Make a Million;* and *Joys of Oral Love.*

These titles are, taken together, mildly amusing, but some
of the humor is drained from them when one considers that,
in the same Marboro mailing, are also listed remaindered
books by George Bernard Shaw, Thomas Mann, Hugo von
Hofmannsthal, André Malraux, D. H. Lawrence, Lewis Car-
roll, Günter Grass, Sholem Aleichem, Aleksandr Solzhenitsyn, and Bertrand Russell. The point is plain: Gresham's
point about the bad driving out the good. The fact is that
publishers' hunches, often distorted into canards, have real
literary consequences. A publishing canard circulated in recent years, for example, has it that books of short stories do
not sell. The result is that they are rarely published, and
then usually only if their authors have an established reputation. The effect is that writers put less energy, because less
hope, into their short stories. Fewer good stories get written.
The loser is literature.

Where once there were a number of serious publishers,

today the field is filled with that very different thing, "general publishers," firms that bring out good and bad books alike. In part this is owing to the emergence and rise of the university presses, upon which publishers can now shuck off their earlier commitment to publish a more regular diet of serious books. Their assumption is that certain books of serious subject and high quality, but small commercial possibility, are best brought out for a limited audience by university presses. But the problem here is that much good writing—works of belle-lettristic history, poetry, essays—falls between the two stools of commercial and scholarly publishing. The consequences for literature once again are depressing, especially for writers who make up the variegated bulk of lesser literary genius. The situation bodes the demise of the quiet yet distinguished minor literary career. If Max Beerbohm, Ronald Firbank, and Maurice Baring were alive and writing in America today, they would be hard pressed to find publishers willing to bring out their work. So, too, if they were beginning their careers, would Edmund Wilson and Lionel Trilling, whose works were preponderantly essays.

If readers grow confused by the mad proliferation of book titles in current-day publishing, bookstore owners, by their own admission, are often scarcely less so. A few years ago in *The New Yorker*, Bruce Bliven, Jr., wrote about the workaday life of a commission book salesman in the South and Southwest. Not least of the fascinating revelations in the article is how little time a salesman can spend talking with the owner of a bookstore about any single title—generally, as it turns out, less than a minute. But this is much facilitated, for salesman and store owner alike, if a book has what is known in the trade as a "handle," a sentence or two by which the salesman can succinctly summarize and sell the book. Because neither the salesman nor the owner can find time to read anywhere near all the books he sells, the handle comes in—well, handy. When my own book came out, my editor called, in some desperation, to see if we couldn't between us find a handle for it. A sales meeting was coming up and the fate of the book, as of any book, was inextricably involved in selling the salesmen on its salability. We never did find a good handle for my book, a fact to which the box under my desk stands in mute testimony.

Does all this suggest that only the most trashy literature will rise to the top? Not at all. Out of the vast confusion in publishing, anything and everything can rise to the top. A few years ago, Gore Vidal wrote an essay entitled "The Top Ten Sellers" in which he reviewed the novels then on the best-seller list. His intention was to show that best-selling novels were those that embodied the fantasies and idiot preoccupations of Americans, and especially the American romance with the movies. But something more complicated is involved. For a book, fiction or nonfiction, to make the best-seller list is not (as was once thought) a guarantee of its unseriousness. Among contemporary writers, Saul Bellow, Mary McCarthy, Aleksandr Solzhenitsyn, John Cheever, Irving Howe, and Gore Vidal himself have written books that turned out to be best sellers. Among earlier writers, George Santayana, George Orwell, and Richard Wright had books chosen as main selections of the Book-of-the-Month Club.

Can a publisher create a best seller out of whole cloth (and afterward out of paperback)? This is a subject much in the flux of controversy. My own view is that publishers cannot do it so easily as one might think. For a book to sell in the hundreds of thousands, a sizable market has to exist; and publishers, although they generally do not want for cynicism, do not always know their markets so well as they would like others to believe. The success of *Jonathan Livingston Seagull* could not have been predicted, nor could that of Erich Segal's *Love Story*. Such books cannot be deliberately manufactured or faked; one must truly feel the meretricious emotions that went into their making. The wide sale of some books, however—or at least the chance of their selling wide-

ly—is predictable. The author who has struck the gong once
figures to strike it a second and third and fourth time, having already built up a following. Books on social problems,
preferably written by M.D.s or psychologists with doctor-
ates, that tell people to do exactly as they want to do any-
how (*Everything You Always Wanted To Know About Sex but
Were Afraid To Ask* and *Creative Divorce* are two examples)
have an excellent chance of being ridden into the winners'
circle. Books of popular psychology that allow for plenty of
party chat—such as Gail Sheehy's *Passages*—are always
strong contenders, as are thrillers that can be read in a
single sitting (*Jaws*).

For more serious books to catch commercial fire, a fortunate concatenation of events must occur. Sometimes a book
will appear at precisely the right time, catching the wind of
the *Zeitgeist* and taking off into the Valhalla of best-seller-
dom. Alex Haley's *Roots* appears to have been such a book.
Sometimes, after a long career, a writer, particularly a novelist, will, as if from heaven, get the call. He appears on the
cover of *Time* or *Newsweek;* front-page reviews of his book
appear everywhere; he becomes the subject of interviews;
People works him up into a photographic profile. (Such, of
late, seems to have been the case with John Cheever.) Sometimes, though, the same treatment can backfire, as it did two
decades ago with James Gould Cozzens, a distinguished
writer who got the call—*Time* cover and the rest—with *By
Love Possessed*, his least distinguished book. After all the
hoopla, the inevitable reaction set in. One attack in particular, a devastation by Dwight Macdonald entitled "By Cozzens Possessed," jolted James Gould Cozzens's reputation so
severely that even now, two decades later, it has not yet
recovered. Sometimes an excellent novel will nearly expire
for want of attention—Walker Percy's first novel, *The Movie-
goer*, is a prime example—then at the last moment will be
pulled back from the flood of oblivion by winning a significant literary prize. After selling scarcely at all, *The Movie-*

goer won in 1961, the year it was published, the then quite prestigious National Book Award.

But how arbitrary it all is! How madcap and how sad! It is not, one suspects, that many good books go unpublished; it is, rather, that they tend to get lost amid the rubbish of so many bad books. Something like 40,000 titles are currently issued in the course of a year in the United States; and the number of books intended for general bookstores, excluding textbooks and scholarly works, is now four times greater than the number published twenty-five years ago. The result is that the stock in bookstores is continually changing. The lives of good books are shortened: six or seven months after a book has been published, if it is not a brisk seller, it disappears from the shelves of even well and intelligently stocked bookstores. Either a book makes it fast or it tends not to make it at all. From the standpoint of an author, as Sybille Bedford has recently remarked, publishing today is all serve and volley.

I had an early taste of the effects of the changed publishing atmosphere some while ago when I was working on a political magazine that, as a special project, brought out a paperback book about the Soviet Union which we hoped to sell on the mass market. At that time the book cost roughly ten cents a copy to manufacture. Thinking that the more reasonably priced the book was, the better its chances of selling, we priced it at sixty cents a copy. The effect was to kill the book instantly. Why? Because we had not counted on the competition for shelf space. No paperback seller wished to stock so low-priced a book. Why should he, when the same space could carry a paperback priced at $1.25? That was in 1964. Today the same book, which would probably cost forty cents a copy to manufacture, would doubtless have to be priced at $2.95 a copy to have a chance.

Of late it has become convenient to blame the troubles of publishing on conglomerates, which in recent years have bought up more and more independent publishing companies. Representative Morris K. Udall has warned that publishing will soon be studied for evidence of monopolistic concentration. The Authors' Guild has meanwhile urged the government to halt the "sinister process" of mergers in publishing. Publishers owned by conglomerates insist that there is nothing amiss here. "Why shouldn't Gulf & Western be allowed to own a publishing company?" an officer of a publishing company owned by Gulf & Western asked not long ago. "They don't bother us editorially." While ownership by conglomerates doubtless does exert additional pressures for profit, and in the crunch perhaps crucial pressures, I, for one, believe him. I only wish that someone *would* bother publishers editorially.

"At last," runs an ad in *Publishers Weekly*, "the definitive Christian sex manual." The book being advertised is titled *Intended for Pleasure: Sex Techniques and Sexual Fulfillment in Christian Marriage*. Do I sound too much like Pontius Pilate if I ask, Who are these Christians? Do they have a need for such a book? Or is it only, once again, a publisher trying to hit a fairly large market—Christians who copulate? "At last," runs an ad in the *New York Times*, "a Mafia wife 'talks'!" Who invited her to talk? The answer, I should guess, is a publisher, or an author hot on the trail of publication, at whose end he espies El Dorado. "Why some people are luckier than others and how you can become one of them," runs an ad for a book entitled *The Luck Factor*. "Get lucky," the ad concludes. "Get *The Luck Factor*. Today." But is it not really the publisher, and the author along with him, who sit with their fingers crossed, themselves hoping to get lucky with this book?

By the time you read this, all three of these books should be on their way to Marboro Country. But perhaps one of them will prove a winner. (Forced to choose, my money would ride on the Christian sex manual.) When they feel called upon to do so, publishers justify such books—"nonbooks," they are rightly termed, denoting that they have no

standing as true books—by saying that they often help pay
the way for more distinguished work that, because it is distinguished, does not figure to pay for itself. Not all publishers count on long shots coming in. Some derive substan-
tial profits from publishing textbooks or reference works;
others, a steady income from a solid backlist; a very few,
from carefully publishing good books. But most publishers,
if they can have one or two big winners a season, can afford
to stay in the game.

That publishing has increasingly become a game, a heady
and enticing game for some of its principal players, is no
longer in doubt. Yet it is not a game without victims. Some
of these victims are good bookstores, which are gradually
being squeezed out by the literary supermarkets such as
Kroch's, Waldenbooks, and Dalton's; good books, which too
often get lost in the shuffle and drowned out in the din; and
readers, whose tastes are not cultivated but confused by the
profusion of caviar and slops heaped together before them
on a single platter.

The solution, easier advised than accomplished, is to publish fewer books. How might this be done? Should authors
be offered grants for *not* writing books, as farmers are
offered subsidies for letting their fields lie fallow? Or what
about publishing books that go directly from the printer to
the remainder stores, thereby saving the expense of selling
and handling in regular bookstores? Or should publishers
invoke standards instead of believing in canards and following hunches, agreeing to publish only those books that demonstrate genuine literary talent or a thoughtful approach to
serious intellectual and social questions? That this last possibility seems quite as unlikely as the other two is a measure
of how far the game of publishing has gotten out of hand.

Incidental Meditations

Does anyone in America like his or her life? I assume not many people do, basing this assumption on the peculiar quality of the endless stream of how-to books that continue to appear in our country. There can, after all, be no thriving how-to literature unless there is a furious want-to feeling abroad in the land. What people want, this literature indicates, is to change their lives. Whereas our earlier how-to literature featured succeeding and getting on in the world—from Benjamin Franklin's *The Way to Wealth* through Dale Carnegie's *How To Win Friends and Influence People*—our current how-to literature features learning how to cope with life through solving our problems. While the former was crudely moral in tone, the tone of the latter is almost exclusively psychological. Every day and in every way, these books cumulatively postulate, we are getting worse and worse. But help is at hand. These books promise to save our marriages or make easier our divorces, redeem our children, give meaning to our work, enhance our sex lives, get us in better touch with our bodies, teach us how to die, and withal bring us through the valley of the shadow of anomie to the gates of the heavenly city here on earth, over which, in neon, is spelled out the single word—fulfillment.

If these books are any reflection of the quality of our lives, we are in one hell of a shape. We have problems. We have the problem of child rearing and the problem of aging, the problem of youth and the problem of dying. In between we have the problems of marriage, family, and sex. Then we have the problem of work and the problem of leisure. This is not to speak of the problems of adjustment of various kinds, the special problems of women, and the problem of retirement, nor of the problems somewhat more external to us: of politics, technology, ecology. So many problems, indeed, there seems little time left over for living. They are a problem, no doubt about it, these problems.

How did all these problems—the problem problem, so to say—come about? Difficult to say. Which came first—the Oedipus complex or Dr. Freud, bad sex or Dr. David Reuben telling us that much better sex awaits our mastering his catechism? Is life substantively worse, more problem-ridden, now than ever before? Or is it that, life having become substantively better, we now have more time to devote to our problems? Is democracy to blame for imbuing people with an inflated sense of their possibilities? One cannot, for example, suffer the problem of feeling powerless if one does not believe oneself entitled to feel powerful to begin with. Has industrial capitalism caused the withering away of the old supports: the family, the neighborhood, the church? Whatever is the cause, whoever is to blame, the important fact is that many good and intelligent people feel themselves sinking under the weight of their problems, and life generally seems less good.

Yet one cannot help wondering to what extent our suffering is linked to the way we perceive all our various problems. Whether or not they have read Freud or others of the Viennese delegation, the way most people nowadays perceive their problems, indeed their lives generally, is in the therapeutic mode. A few years ago Philip Rieff, the sociologist and interpreter of the works of Sigmund Freud, wrote a book with the prophetic title of *The Triumph of the Therapeutic.* I say "prophetic" because it now seems obvious that the therapeutic, as a mode of viewing the world and one's own place in it, has completely triumphed, and in America at present we are living in a state of unconditional surrender to it. With the aid of therapeutic ideas and notions, we are able to cultivate our problems with a refinement perhaps unknown to any other nation in history. We have become connoisseurs of grievance—one nation problematical, with anxiety and aggravation for all.

What is the therapeutic mode of perceiving the world? In its broadest lineaments, it is seated in the interior, a view that what is most significant in life is played out in one's mind. Played out is accurate, for the therapeutic mode provides those who adopt it a way of dramatizing their lives. Its key metaphors are turmoil, crisis, struggle, and breakthrough: Oedipal turmoil, identity crisis, struggle between id and superego, conscious and unconscious, Eros and Thanatos. The breakthrough, the denouement in this drama, if it arrives, is greater self-knowledge, awareness, growth, fulfillment. Men have availed themselves of other dramas—the Jewish messianic drama, the Protestant drama of salvation—but the therapeutic drama as generally conceived is notable in being a play with a cast of one: one's self.

The chief playwright in the therapeutic drama was of course Sigmund Freud, and in *Civilization and Its Discontents* he left very clear stage instructions that it is to be played with tragic overtones. The road company version that has appeared in America, however, has largely ignored these instructions, and the script has been played in a rewritten version that has a happy ending. Much speculative thought has been lavished on why Freudianism and the therapeutic mode have caught on in the United States as nowhere else. No reason has ever seemed as persuasive as that they are particularly well suited to the American belief in personal progress and the endless alterability of character—a belief simultaneously responsible for much of our stupidity and much of our decency. Ours is pre-eminently the country of the second chance—and the third and the fourth and the fifth. As the game is not over till the gun goes off, so in America our character, our life, is still deemed reformable so long as we draw breath. What makes the therapeutic mode so appealing is precisely that it holds out hope for personal change. Freud wrote: "Much is won if we succeed in transforming hysterical misery into common unhappiness." Here in America we have read him to mean that happiness is just around the corner.

Not that the therapeutic mode has wanted for detractors, who over the years have come not only from philistine but from intellectual quarters. Karl Kraus led the Viennese opposition in writing: "The relation between psychiatrists and other kinds of lunatic is more or less the relation of a convex folly to a concave one." Vladimir Nabokov, who saw the determinism inherent in the therapeutic enterprise as repugnant to the artistic enterprise, once said: "Let the credulous and the vulgar continue to believe that all mental woes can be cured by a daily application of old Greek myths to their private parts. I really do not care." Opinion about psychiatrists, psychoanalysts, and psychologists today seems a highly mixed one. In one of their aspects, they are our secular priests, consulted on matters private and public, minor and major alike; but in another of their aspects they are figures of fun, incompetents blinkered by obtuse doctrine, even slightly charlatan. A winning television situation comedy, *The Bob Newhart Show*, featured a psychologist who is decent but clearly bumbling and ineffectual; in this show, the very idea of psychotherapy was itself treated as situation comedy. Even people who are in therapy of one kind or another are frequently ironic about it. In the work of Woody Allen, so much of which is psychoanalytic in inspiration, irony mounts to hilarity.

Still, the efficacy of the therapeutic mode is not in doubt. People who have undergone psychotherapy of one kind or another insist that it has changed their lives. Some say that it has in fact saved their lives. Others maintain that talking to a therapist has brought welcome surcease from oppressive problems. Who can refute such claims? Who, moreover, can refute that the findings of psychiatry, along with those of psycho-pharmacology, have improved enormously the treatment of the psychotic, the tempering of the neurotic, and the running of institutions for the mentally ill? It is owing to such findings that the days of dank dungeons and the dish under the door for the insane are over, and that is something to be grateful for.

Yet what of the effect of these same psychological findings—the large theories and the small scraps of information—on the conduct of everyday life? If modern psychology has in many instances made the neurotic well, in how many others has it made the well neurotic? This cannot of course be known. What can is that psychology, the therapeutic mode, has permeated nearly every aspect of public and private life in our time. In the public realm, most social movements in recent years have been, or soon become, therapeutic in their demands. The civil rights movement became therapeutic at exactly that moment when it ceased to talk of legal and economic problems and took up "Black is beautiful" as one of its chief slogans. The movements on behalf of women and homosexuals, once each affixed the word "liberation" to its cause, staked out demands that are largely therapeutic as well, making clear that it is liberation from a psychologically repressed status that they seek. Much of the talk about ethnicity soon shades off into the therapeutic, with group identity the main theme.

In the private realm, the influence of the therapeutic mode has been at once more subtle and more pervasive. It has infiltrated the modern vocabulary and taken over wide areas of modern thought. It has made analysts of us all, searching literature, our friends, our selves for motives and the wizardry of the unconscious at its devious work. In a speech at a dinner in Vienna honoring Sigmund Freud on his eightieth birthday, Thomas Mann correctly cited Freud as an "artist of thought, like Schopenhauer, and like him a writer of the European rank." "Freud is of the opinion," Mann added, "that the significance of psychoanalysis as a science of the unconscious will in the future far outrank its value as a therapeutic method." Mann thought that this new science would result in a "humanism of the future," in a "wise and freer humanity"—"freed from fear and hate, and ripe for peace." In short, by eating from this new tree of knowledge we were to be returned to Eden.

Mann's speech was delivered in 1936. Thirty-odd years later, in *Mr. Sammler's Planet*, Saul Bellow has a character say to Artur Sammler: "I'm convinced that knowing the names of things braces people up. I've gone to shrinkers for years, and have they cured me of anything? They have not. They've put labels on my troubles, though, which sound like knowledge. It's a great comfort and worth the money. You say 'I'm manic.' Or you say 'I'm a reactive-depressive.'. . . Then the dullest brain has internal fireworks, and the sparks drive you out of your skull. It's divine. You think you're a new man."

At a minimum, after confronting Freud in any of his major works, the tendency is to think oneself a different man. Thomas Mann said of the analytic revelation that "once aroused and on the alert, it cannot be put to sleep again," and how accurate that statement is. Having recently read Freud's *The Psychopathology of Everyday Life*, I am convinced that one of its effects is to make everyday life more psychopathological. That book, it will be recalled, is the one in which Freud takes up such matters as forgetting, slips of the tongue, misreadings and slips of the pen, bungled actions, errors, and other parapraxes, or faulty functions, among people not otherwise psychically troubled. Made up for the most part of small case studies, instances of everyday behavior—many of them observed by Freud, and others reported by his psychoanalytic cohorts—the book is by and large not one of Freud's better performances. Still, it is Freud's, and therefore has much peripheral wisdom to convey, such as that contained in his analogy between the screen memories of childhood and the store of myths and legends of its early days that a nation acquires as it grows older.

"You Freudians," Freud records a lady saying to his colleague Ferenczi, "will go on looking for the causes of insanity till you're insane yourselves." Much that appears patent madness is in these pages. *"In every case,"* writes Freud, after citing a number of examples of forgetting, *"the forgetting turned out to be based on a motive of unpleasure,"* and later, "nothing is ever mislaid except as a result of unconscious intention." Of the quite commonly bungled action in which one tries to step around someone approaching on a sidewalk, then that person steps the same way, so that one is engaged with a stranger in a comic minuet, Freud remarks that here "behind a mask of clumsiness, [one] pursues sexual aims." Not only is losing objects ascribed to psychological motives, but, according to Otto Rank, "also *finding* them appears to be [psychologically] determined." No move is arbitrary or random; there are no accidents.

Freud is almost everywhere a brilliantly clever polemicist—he had, after all, an extraordinary case to make—and is therefore sometimes quite difficult to pin down. Often he will make bold statements, only later to send in sentries of qualification to guard them. But in *The Psychopathology of Everyday Life* he is quite clear on the point of our actions being determined. "If we give way to the view that a part of our psychical functioning cannot be explained by purposive ideas," he writes, "we are failing to appreciate the extent of determination in mental life." And he ends his book on everyday slips and forgetting and small errors by writing: *"the phenomenon can be traced back to incompletely suppressed psychical material, which, although pushed away by consciousness, has nevertheless not been robbed of all capacity of expressing itself."* Case closed.

Part of Freud's genius is in his extraordinary power of suggestiveness. Of one of the cases mentioned in *The Psychopathology of Everyday Life,* an instance of symptomatic acts, Freud reports: "I had been telling the patient about such chance or symptomatic acts only the evening before. She thereupon took the first opportunity of producing something analogous." If a great teacher is one who sets others off on his own train of thought, then Freud is probably the greatest teacher of all time. No one provides a more entrancing—if not always enchanting—ride. After reading the chapter in *The Psychopathology of Everyday Life* on "Forgetting Proper Names," I turned on the television set for the evening news, whereupon a singer appeared doing a commercial for Burlington Industries. I knew this singer's name very well, but could not, no matter how strenuous my efforts, bring it to mind. Only hours later was I able to recall that her name is Petula Clark. Significance please? Miss Clark does not even faintly resemble my mother, and I have no sisters, so perhaps it would be best to rule out incest taboos from the start. Miss Clark once made a successful recording of a song entitled "Downtown." I do not go downtown much any more. Ought I to? Is there some dark secret connected with downtown that I am repressing? My dentist is downtown, but I do not need the help of my unconscious to repress him. This little incident of forgetting could take years in the unraveling. What, I wonder, would be the significance of my forgetting the whole thing, which I most certainly intend to do?

Because psychotherapy over the past few decades has been so popular among the middle classes, perhaps everyone who is among those classes has heard, or told, wondrous stories about their own or other people's therapeutic adventures. My own favorite—told to me at third or fourth hand, and hence possibly apocryphal—has to do with a famous American sculptor and an equally famous psychoanalyst. The sculptor had recently been divorced, was in heavy debt, and found himself in a terrible general funk, which he sought to alleviate through the ministrations of the psychoanalyst. When he called at the analyst's office, the analyst invited him to join him on his habitual post-prandial walk in a nearby park, where he, the sculptor, might tell him about his problems. Upon their return, at the entrance to his office, the analyst said to the sculptor: "My dear sir, it strikes me that you have two reigning problems. The first is that you need a woman. The second is that you need money. I am afraid that I am able to aid you with neither. So let us say good-day here, and I wish you all good luck."

What I like about this story, I do not mind admitting, is its anti-therapeutic bias. What I find appealing about it is its frank admission that not all human problems are linked to childhood memories, sexual complications, or one form or another of repression. It also somewhat obliquely incorporates the thought in a sentence by Cesare Pavese that I find most interesting but to which I am not sure many people would any longer lend their assent: "One ceases to be a child when one realizes that telling one's troubles does not make them any better." As for why I have come to hold an anti-therapeutic bias, the reasons are many, but chief among them is my belief that the therapeutic mode does not now come anywhere near achieving its own pretensions to explaining the totality of human experience. I would go further to say that I believe it is helpless to explain what is most interesting in human experience.

Imagine, then, my immense pleasure at discovering my bias against the therapeutic mode more sharply formulated than I could ever hope to formulate it and having it done in a book by, of all people, a practicing academic psychologist. The book is *Human Beings* by Liam Hudson. Although more than solely a debunking performance, Professor Hudson's book is most impressive on the attack—best at pointing out what really is not known. Of psychological research to date he writes: "The contours are there, we feel, all the outward signs. But the sense of fabric itself, its real stuff and substance, is missing." What is most sorely missing, in both the Freudian and the behavioristic psychological models, is any convincing account of the concepts of will and imagination. Will and imagination, the factors responsible for heroism, altruism, and art, among much else, are surely two of the most important elements in life, yet in modern psychology both are, implicitly and sometimes explicitly, degraded— will being chalked off to determinism and imagination to sublimated fantasy.

Ought we, for example, to regard Aleksandr Solzhenitsyn's conduct as a classic case of revolt from an authoritarian father (Stalin)? Was not Nadezhda Mandelstam, in carrying around in her head for decades her husband Osip's poems— the sublimated products of his fantasies?—acting out the traditionally subservient role of women? What of Martin Luther King, Jr.'s, or for that matter Sigmund Freud's, courage in the teeth of adversity—can these be adequately accounted for by a psychological analysis of their childhoods, sexualities, even genetic inheritances? The therapeutic mode makes not only evil but heroism banal. Here I am reminded of a passage from André Malraux's *The Walnut Trees of Altenberg:*

> "Essentially a man is what he hides . . ."
> Walter shrugged his shoulders and brought his hands together like a child making a mud pie.
> "A man is what he does!" my father answered sharply.

If the therapeutic mode can make the heroic seem banal, it often makes ordinary human suffering seem positively trivial. Anyone of any intelligence who has gone through any form of personal upheaval in this country in recent years— divorce, difficulties with children, the death of someone loved—cannot but feel the sting of triviality visited upon his very real problems by the therapeutic mode. Whatever one's suffering, a psychologist stands ready to explain it (or explain it away), several books have been written about it, an article on it has appeared in one of the Sunday supplements,

Time or *Newsweek* has done it up in a brisk six hundred words. After hearing them often enough, one eventually becomes hostage to certain psychological clichés. A man's wife divorces him, and he accounts for it as the result of the "liberation thing." A woman loses a husband after forty years of marriage, and for more than a year afterward breaks into tears at odd moments, which her children, of the therapeutically enlightened generation, diagnose as "the widow syndrome." Thus do forty years of life go up in the smoke of a cheap little phrase.

The psychologist's job, as Professor Hudson puts it, "is to make sense of people's biographies." But one nowadays wonders if psychologists have not made rather too much sense of them—like a Chinese laundry of the mind, boiling out the stains and flattening life's interesting wrinkles. Not only has psychology in its application to daily life succeeded in divesting life of much of its rich complication, but it has gone further to persuade people of the truth of its rather crude simplicities. Professor Hudson remarks that "while psychologists may have had little direct experimental influence over what people do, there can be not the slightest doubt that we have contributed in a massive way to what they believe." Psychologists, both academic and clinical, are in his view "engaged in psychic engineering: in the alteration of human consciousness."

Engineering is apt from another vantage, and this is as a reflection of the industrialization of psychology, and hence of the therapeutic mode of viewing the world, that has taken place in the United States in recent years. We have in America what can only be called a discontent industry. Psychoanalytic institutes, psychologists of various schools in various kinds of private practice, the strange cluster of the desperately hopeful gathered under the banner of the human potential movement, transcendental meditation centers—these are but a handful of the psychic comfort stations dotted across our nation. A book on marriage counseling, *The Marriage*

Savers by Joanne and Lew Koch, discusses, among other therapeutic techniques used by marriage counselors, bioenergetics, psychodramas, transactional analysis, kin network therapy, group sex therapy, encounter groups, and sex surrogates. Then there are the books offering every possible psychological nostrum from Nena and George O'Neill's *Open Marriage* to Jerry Greenwald's *Creative Intimacy*. In her novel about Marin County, *The Serial*, Cyra McFadden has a character who, over the years, has tried "Gurdjieff, Silva Mind Control, actualism, analytical tracking, parapsychology, Human Life Styling, postural integration, the Fischer-Hoffman Process, hatha and raja yoga, integral massage, orgonomy, palmistry, Neo-Reichian bodywork and Feldenkrais functional integration." The discontent industry, like the auto industry, offers something for every taste and budget. How much money is spent annually on discontent in the United States is not known, but it must be considerable. As advertising used to be credited with creating new needs, one now wonders if the discontent industry does not have a stake in creating new problems. With the economy in the shape it is in, one wonders, too, if we can afford much in the way of contentment.

It would be nice to think that one can remain aloof from all this, not participating in it in any way, but enjoying the spectacle, the circus quality of it all, with a fine Menckenesque disdain. But such disdain does not figure to work for long; the therapeutic mode has seeped too deeply into public and private life for it not to influence us all. What is the appropriate response to books and articles and personal conversations that postulate that our technology is symbolic of our national death wish, or that the assassination of political leaders in America is an obvious acting out of the wish to murder the father? How is one to react when told by one's child's school guidance counselor that perhaps the girl is "role- as opposed to goal-oriented"? What say to the blather of therapeutic language that clogs public discourse and private talk, with words like "meaningful," "growthful," "identity crisis," and "relate to" spattering the walls. So much garbage in the air, yet no one moves to turn off the fans.

A common thread runs through much of this, and though it can perhaps be traced back to Rousseau and Nietzsche (who once referred to himself as "the first psychologist of Europe"), it is unmistakable in Freud, and much more so among the workers in the therapeutic vineyards who have followed him. The common thread is the idea that people are essentially driven rather than driving, acted upon rather than active agents in their own destinies. In Freud it is the unconscious that is driving us. In others who have taken Freud's ideas over into social and political realms, it is institutions or technology or history that is doing the driving. Having these ideas dinned into us with sufficient regularity, most of us are ready to turn over the wheel.

Meanwhile, many reach out for each new set of therapeutic safety belts that is put on the market: assertiveness training, alpha wave control, biorhythms, transcendental meditation, scientology, Erhard Seminar Training (EST). The books roll out: *The High-Fibre Way to Total Health, The Bhagavad Gita for Daily Living, The Handbook to Higher Consciousness. From Sad to Glad, Positive Prayers for Powerful Living, Death: The Final Stage of Growth*—you name it, kid, we got it. What is more, so long as the therapeutic mode rides supreme, we can expect a lot more of it.

In discussing what he describes as "essential tensions," Professor Hudson writes: "To conceive of them [tensions] within the quasi-technological rhetoric of 'problem-solving' is to abandon whatever purchase upon them we might possess. The belief, implicit in the idea of progress, that a good life lies ahead of us—a good life that is our rightful inheritance and that we can reach by solving our problems— seems to me a specious fiction." The point is not that the problems we live with are not real—they often are, crushingly so—it is that the therapeutic mode so frequently trivializes them that in many of its contemporary aspects the therapeutic mode is itself part of the problem.

Part of what is required is a lowering of the national consciousness, a slipping away from the therapeutic mode. When it is possible to do so, what a relief it is to throw the ideas of the therapeutic mode off. The other day a friend, after detailing the habitually wretched behavior of a colleague, remarked, in psychological extenuation of this behavior, that of course he had had a terribly troubled childhood. "If his childhood was so troubled," I found myself replying, "why doesn't he consider growing up?" But old habits die hard. Freud said that to "interpret one's dreams demands a high degree of self-discipline." To extricate oneself from the assumptions of the therapeutic mode, so long and so deeply ingrained in modern life have they become, perhaps requires even more.

We might commence with language. Wherever possible, replace the word "guilt" with "conscience," "personality" with "character." Banish "syndrome," "latent," and "complex." "Fulfillment" and "creative," in their therapeutic usages, would make fine subtractions. Once upon a time it could be said, as Sir Maurice Bowra put it, that the ideas of the therapeutic mode "gave a new dimension to talk about character and behavior." But that was in the 1920s. It is no longer so. They have become boring, if not otiose. Bad language partly got us into this; perhaps straight language can help get us out.

In a quite mindless book by Adam Smith entitled *Powers of the Mind*, I came across another aid to releasing oneself from bondage to the therapeutic mode. The author directed my attention to the work of one Herbert Benson, M.D., associate professor at the Harvard Medical School and director of the hypertension section of Boston's Beth Israel Hospital. Dr. Benson has devised a method of having his high blood pressure patients sit in a comfortable position in a quiet place while breathing through the nose and repeating a one-syllable word of their own choosing for a period of twenty minutes twice daily. Apparently, this almost unfailingly brings down blood pressure, and in the process creates a welcome feeling of restfulness. Dr. Benson has published his findings in a modest little book entitled *The Relaxation Response.*

Although I do not have high blood pressure, I have been doing Dr. Benson's exercise off and on for roughly the past two months, and I find it, as advertised, refreshingly restful. I would estimate that it has changed my life by as much as .008 percent, though possibly I overestimate. The relaxation response is a spin-off of sorts from the technique used in transcendental meditation, minus the $125 fee and the mystical trappings involved in the latter. Having no hunger for mystical experience, life at the quotidian being mysterious enough for me, I call my adaptation of Dr. Benson's technique Incidental Meditation, and use the time allotted for it to think about exclusively pleasant things. Sitting in a comfortable wing chair, my feet on a coffee table, doing my breathing, I think about autumn leaves burning at dusk, a tranquil green lake in Wisconsin, gulls in flight, birch trees, a tennis court in the rain, a puppy bounding, lofty spiral football passes thrown by a chubby thirteen-year-old named Bobby Rubenstein, William Hazlitt's gravestone upon which is engraved the words "Contented and Grateful," landscapes in England, herds of giraffes cantering off into the distance.

Although all thoughts in the therapeutic mode are outlawed from these restful reveries, the mind being a great wanderer, as one of the famous mystics once put it, on occasion Dr. Freud drops in for a visit. He sets down his umbrella, takes a seat on the couch across from my wing chair, and lights up a cigar. We fall into easy conversation. "So," he says, "tell me, is this true about there being sex surrogates in California?" It is true, I tell him. "Sex surrogates," he says, "women who sleep with men for money under the aegis of the therapeutic! In Vienna they had a different name for such women.... And what about this organization, EST?" he asks. "Is it true they will not allow people out of the room, once their sessions begin, not even to relieve themselves?" "It is true, or so I have read, Doctor." After answering other of his questions about additional bizarreries performed in the name of the therapeutic, Dr. Freud begins softly to sob. "It did not have to be like this," he says. "The idea was to relieve misery, not to enact such pathetic clownishness." In my reverie, I go over to him and pat him gently on the shoulder, murmuring, "There, there, Doctor, there, there." But try though I do, I cannot bring myself to lie to him and say, "None of this is your fault."

Dandies Askew

Right up there on the scale of boring things to do, alongside telling stories of one's sexual conquests and reporting on the scholastic achievements of one's children, is recounting one's dreams. At the risk of boring, then, I have a dream to recount—a nightmare, as it turns out. I am driving on the San Diego Freeway in Los Angeles when an enormous truck pushes my car, a rented Mercedes convertible, over to the side of the road, and thence over a guardrail, from where I plunge to my death. My body, which is sent from the Los Angeles County morgue to a local funeral home, is badly burned, though the features of my face are still recognizable. The director of the funeral home telephones my family, informing them that he will be pleased to prepare their loved one for burial. This they, my grieving family, give him permission to do. My clothes have been burned in the car crash and so has my hair. The funeral director has no photograph of me, but he can make out that I, the deceased, was a man of early middle age. He determines to dress me for burial in what, in Los Angeles, is his estimation of the style of the day.

Here the nightmare begins in earnest. First he fits me out in a wig, a tight little helmet of black hair, which covers my ears and comes down in soft bangs on my forehead. He slides a flowery shirt over my torso, leaving the top three buttons undone. Around my neck he attaches two gold chains, one with a symbol of my religious faith, the other with my astrological sign. My body is next slipped into a denim suit, with prominent orange stitching and lavish bell-bottom trousers. On my feet he places boots of a crinkly black patent leather with gold buckles. Whether to paste a Fu Manchu or a Zapata mustache across my lip or to leave it naked is a decision, he feels, that can await the arrival of my family. As a finishing touch, he puts a large gold digital watch upon my left wrist—a watch that is, quite properly, self-winding.

Since having had that nightmare, I have intended to add a codicil to my will. I have formulated this codicil only in rough draft; no doubt a legal hand will be required to put it in final form. But here is what I have in mind:

"Should the deceased die before the age of fifty, he wishes to be buried in a blue blazer with dull gold buttons, dark gray trousers, and Bass Weejun loafers (black or cordovan brown, color optional). His socks should be black and should ride up over the calf; his shirt be solid white or light blue and of a durable oxford cloth, though if neither of these is ready to hand, a stripe of conservative tendency will do. If a striped shirt is chosen, he wishes to be buried wearing a necktie of solid color, something lively but not obstreperous—a maroon, say, or possibly a forest green or a quiet yellow; if a solid-color shirt is available, he wishes to be buried wearing a striped tie or one of subdued challis pattern. He wishes no jewelry to go with him (arrangements for disposal of his wristwatch and the pocket watch of his grandfather are made elsewhere in this document). The same goes for hair: he demands to be buried with whatever hair he has remaining atop his head cut short and parted on the right side, and his face to be clean of sideburns, earlocks, muttonchops, mustache of any shape or variety, beard, goatee, or imperial. If the deceased is over fifty years of age, he wishes all the above to apply, except that in place of blazer and trousers he prefers to be buried in a suit of either blue or dark gray. In setting out these instructions, he would have it known that he wants to depart this earth in the style he has lived upon it: that is to say, square, utterly square, but square after his own fashion. Although his good deeds have been few, he nevertheless does not choose to risk having God fail to recognize him."

Oh vanity, thy name is Epstein! But mine is, I believe, vanity of a special (though scarcely unique) kind: the vanity of a man who, above all, does not wish to appear vain. Not all male vanity is of this kind. Alongside male birds like myself, who prefer to travel in camouflage, others go in for elegant plumage, and most fall somewhere in between. Male vanity is doubtless as various as female vanity, and differs from it chiefly in that men, at least in modern times, have not been allowed to give full vent to their vanity. It has been deemed unmanly to seem to care too much about clothes and appearance generally. Yet rare is the man who can look on with equanimity as his hair falls out or his middle thickens and spreads. The vanity of males, having no obvious or traditional outlet, might just exceed that of females.

Vanity is no doubt worth contemning, except that it is partly allied with curiosity—curiosity about that most continuously fascinating of subjects: oneself. Surely it is a superior cosmic joke that, despite all our attempts at introspection, from astrology to psychoanalysis, none of us truly knows what he looks like. Each of us has probably studied his defects. Oh yes, we can pick ourselves out of a group photograph; nor is it a stranger who stares back, his jaws slathered in soap, out of the shaving mirror. But who with confidence can say of himself or herself, "Mine is a kindly— or intelligent, or elegant, or fascinating—face"? Or who has honesty enough to say of himself or herself, "Mine is a vicious—or ignorant, or coarse, or boring—face"? No face is so grotesque that its owner is not able to find a certain charm in it; no face is so charming that its owner is not able to find a certain grotesqueness in it.

Tolstoy, who had a potato nose and few teeth, spoke with his usual acuity about faces. "It seems to me," he writes, "that what we call beauty in a face lies in the smile; if the smile heightens the charm of the face, the face is a beautiful one; if it does not alter it, the face is ordinary; and if it is spoilt by a smile, it is ugly." Interesting though this is—more than interesting, in my opinion, it is true—nonetheless it is not easily applied to oneself. If you do not believe me, try smiling before a mirror.

If our information about our own faces is imperfect, is what we know about our own bodies that much more exact? Do not most fat men secretly think themselves graceful? Does not the most beautiful woman fear that she, in the matter of figure, has too little of this or too much of the other? A person cannot be too rich or too thin, said Babe Paley, late wife of William Paley, the chairman of the board of CBS, and herself formerly a regular in the pages of women's fashion magazines. Through careful and strenuous diet I once lost twenty-odd pounds, and as a result thought myself wondrously trim; it came as something of a disappointment that others only thought I had a wasting disease.

Getting our physical selves into clear focus is not an easy thing. I recall an occasion, some years ago, when I was got up in a tan corduroy jacket, a plaid shirt, and black knit tie—this at a time when one did not usually wear dark shirts with ties—and considered myself very much in the getup of a literary man: a Czech poet in exile, perhaps, or a minor English novelist of exquisite sensibility. One could probably have heard the air seep out of me when a young woman I was introduced to that day asked if I were a furrier. A fur trapper I could have accepted, but a furrier? I was not at all sure what a furrier looked like, and less sure than ever what I looked like.

Am I alone in this inexact knowledge about my own appearance? I suspect not—a suspicion based on my view of the habiliments my fellow men choose for themselves. I am sitting in the aisle seat at a neighborhood movie theater, watching men walk up and down the aisle before the start of the film. What a parade it is! Here is a man in a velour jump suit, bald but for a ring of gray hair, yet with a fierce set of chin whiskers of the kind the old cartoon-strip character Bathless Groggins used to sport. Down the aisle strides a pudgy young man in cut-off jeans, tennis shoes, tube socks pulled up to the knees, a T-shirt bearing the inscription "I Wanna Be Me," and a hairdo (a permanent?) of careful curls—a white man's version of an Afro (a Caucasio, possibly?). Up comes a man with snowy sideburns three fingers thick, wearing an ultra-suede leisure suit which I have heard described alternately as a "Skokie walking suit" or a "Cleveland." Much denim is seen clambering up and down this aisle, clinging to thighs and bottoms of old and young alike. The hot comb has done its contorting work on many a skull here. (And elsewhere: under President Jimmy Carter we have the first hot comb in the White House; his may be remembered as not the imperial but the hair-styled presidency.) But no sooner does one think that most men are attempting to conceal their baldness than down the aisle lopes a young Negro man who has shaved his head. Now comes a gent in white shoes and, atop red trousers, a white belt—the height, the very Acropolis, of Rotarian haberdashery—yet damned if he isn't wearing a Che Guevara beard: Babbitt and bohemian all in one man.

And what about his nibs, your genial columnist, Brummell-D'Orsay-Baudelaire-Disraeli-Montesquiou-Beerbohm-Epstein? How is he got up for this movie? He is not exactly, it is sad to report, bespoke. In the prose style of the men's fashion magazines, here he is: Epstein prefers casual clothes for a night at the movies. His chino pants are by Ralph Lauren ($60); sandals by Thom McAn ($11.95); socks, since he isn't wearing any, are by nobody ($.00); T-shirt with "Circuit

Court Club" printed over the left breast by a firm ashamed to put its name to it, owning up only to Kodel-Polyester ($3.50); and a jogging jacket borrowed from a son who in turn borrowed it from someone else, by Warm Up Suit (price unknown). This is, remember, a neighborhood theater, and informality of a kind that is possible nowadays seems, if not a great boon, a small yet serious comfort. By contrast, I recall my father, at my age, putting on a tie and suit coat and adjusting the brim of his hat at the mirror near the front door, before going out to the corner drugstore for a newspaper.

As the getup I have just described ought to make sufficiently clear, I make no claims to any standing as an arbiter elegantiarum. I should not, though, mind if we had such a figure about these days. An arbiter elegantiarum on men's clothes might set a standard that one could at least choose to flee from. A magazine called *Gentleman's Quarterly*, which is exclusively given over to men's clothes, exists; it was founded by Arnold Gingrich, who was also the founding editor of *Esquire*. But *GQ*, as the magazine styles itself, does not pass muster; it is arbitrary, all right, but not very elegant. It is in thrall to fashion, which is not always synonymous with style and at the moment seems downright antonymous with style. *GQ*'s September 1978 number, for example, has men in leather trousers, thin ties, fur coats, itchy though neither warm nor suave-looking sweaters. Everywhere in its pages these men stare out, sullen of mien, with their suit and jacket collars turned up. Sometimes they are photographed with women, but they do not seem very interested in these women. Male narcissism seems to reign. Or perhaps they are angry at the ugly clothes they have to wear. *GQ* does not in any case seem a magazine for family men.

Neither, in quite a different way, is *Playboy*, which used fairly regularly to run pieces on men's fashions. Even though one gathers that the ideal *Playboy* reader would be for the better part of his days *sans culotte*, a man named Robert L. Green once advised *Playboy* readers what to put on between matings. Mr. Green has since written a book, *Live with Style*, in which he is described as a "fashion arbiter and consultant." Here, from his book, is a sample of his advice and the tone it comes in:

> It's the total look that counts. Don't hold desperately to an earlier image. What looked chic in the 1930s is a joke today. . . . The distinguished look of the straight-laced 'fifties is boring in the 'seventies. The sterile perfection of "correct" clothes is replaced by doing it your own way. You should be an independent man or woman who is perfectly capable of deciding for yourself what subtle updating you want to bring to your party wardrobe. By all means unbutton your casual shirt if it makes you look sexier but not if you look as if you were going to bed.

This may be sensible as advice goes but it is not to my taste. It is not, for one thing, arbitrary enough; and it is not, for another, well enough written. If one is going to write about style one had best do it with style. Mr. Green's prose is blowsy.

One trap to be avoided in writing about men's clothes is effeminacy. Another is snobbery. Even if one feels clothes are important, it is well to remember that they are not that important. The great cannonade against the interest in male attire is, of course, Thomas Carlyle's *Sartor Resartus*. "A Dandy," Carlyle writes, "is a Clothes-wearing Man, a Man whose trade, office and existence consists in the wearing of Clothes. Every faculty of his soul, spirit, purse and person is heroically consecrated to this one object, the wearing of Clothes wisely and well: so that as others dress to live, he lives to dress." Although Carlyle's has been the most boisterous attack on clothes, a high-minded contempt for clothes has always been part of intellectual tradition—rather as if clothes were too trivial a matter to give time to by people who think great thoughts. Thus Socrates, in Plato, is regularly referred to as wearing his "shabby old mantle." Tolstoy, we know from photographs, paraded about Yasnaya Polyana in the loose blouse and baggy trousers of a peasant. Orwell affected workingmen's tweeds and corduroy trousers.

As contemporary politics ought by now to have taught, style is scarcely ever the man. "Style is the manner of a man or woman or inanimate object. It is never the substance. . . ." That quotation comes from the late George Frazier, the best modern writer on the subject of men's clothes that I have read. Frazier was a columnist for the *Boston Globe*, where he wrote about much else besides clothes, and an entertainment editor at the old *Life*. I used to read him in *Esquire*, where he published articles under such titles as "The Dapper Wrinkles of Seersucker," "Splendor in the Brass" (about English and Scottish uniforms and tailors), and "The Second Greatest Shoeshine in America" (to be had, it turns out, at the airport in Cleveland; the first, or greatest, was a dead-heat tie between the shoe-shine man at the Hotel Pierre and the man at the Waldorf). As befits a man interested in style, George Frazier was himself a stylish character. He would bring his own hot dogs (Tobin's) to football games in Boston, where he paid the concessionaires the regular price of a hot dog to grill them for him. He held conferences with *Esquire* editors in a rowboat in Central Park, for which he packed a lunch of martinis and sandwiches. He wrote an undergraduate essay at Harvard that won the Bowdoin Prize, and bought a suit with the proceeds—a suit that, decade after decade, never ceased to fit him.

George Frazier's own taste in clothes ran to the British and the traditional. ("Dress British and think Yiddish," a recent maxim has it.) His ideal male dressers, apotheoses of masculine elegance, were Fred Astaire, Clark Gable, and William Faulkner; of men of an earlier generation, he approved of Jimmy Walker, the Duke of Windsor, and Herbert Bayard Swope (one of whose neckties was once borrowed for a Broadway play and appropriately credited in the program notes as "on loan from the Herbert Bayard Swope, Sr., col-

lection"). Andy Williams, Johnny Carson, and Leonard Bern-
stein were Frazier's idea of ill-dressed men, or at least men
who did not come off because they failed to understand that
a stylish masculine appearance must never betray the care
taken to achieve it; concern itself must be concealed.

Frazier defined style as "that intangible quality that, at its
most compelling, touches our hearts, arouses our enthusiasm, and sometimes makes us so much its captive that we
can't see straight." Examples of style for George Frazier
were the inflection in Laurence Olivier's voice; Duke Elling-
ton hunched over his piano playing "Satin Doll"; the Balti-
more quarterback Johnny Unitas standing straight up in the
pocket, with would-be tacklers, blood in their eyes, rushing
madly in on him. But if Frazier knew the excitement of style,
he also knew its limitations. He knew style was not character (a higher thing), nor was it fashion (a lower thing).
Style is not the man, yet its presence or absence is part of
the man.

Which part? Not so easily pinned down, to take a trope
from tailoring, yet the clothes a man chooses, or disdains,
are important facets of him. Tolstoy wore the costume of the
peasant and Orwell that of the workingman to show their
contempt for the fripperies of the official dress of the classes
into which each had been born (aristocracy and lower-
upper-middle, respectively). Their choices were far from
negligible, but were political. Tolstoy got up in the finery of
Dickens, with his flamboyant waistcoats, cravats, outsize
cuff links, rings, and the rest, is unthinkable. So, too, is the
prospect of the austere Orwell in the country-gentleman
duds of Evelyn Waugh. Clothes, in these instances, did not
make the men, but they most assuredly were part of them.

Clothes have traditionally functioned as a badge. They
used to tell you where a man stood, sometimes implied his
aspirations, and occasionally conveyed his view of himself.
Especially was this so in large cities. ("In the country," Balzac wrote in *Eugénie Grandet*, "people cease to care about

their appearance. They no longer dress to please others, and eventually become reluctant even to buy a new pair of gloves.") Theodore Dreiser, that great genius-klutz of American fiction, knew what it was to want good clothes; and more than this, within his range he knew the social meaning of clothes with precision. Clothes play a part in all Dreiser's novels, but in *Sister Carrie* so large is the part they play that they nearly qualify as a character. "A woman," Dreiser writes, "should some day write the complete philosophy of clothes. No matter how young, it is one of the things she wholly comprehends. There is an indescribably faint line in the matter of man's apparel which somehow divides for her those who are worth glancing at and those who are not."

Before Dreiser, all the great nineteenth-century novelists dressed out their characters with some care. Closer to our own day, John O'Hara was a writer much interested in clothes. One of his stories was entitled "The Windowpane Check." Another, "The Sharks," begins, "Mr. Plastic Rain Cover for His Hat was taking his daily constitutional." In an O'Hara story it was not unusual to come upon a sentence like the following: "His clothes were perfect; a reddish tweed jacket, sleeveless sweater, tan slacks, Tattersall shirt, knitted necktie." He was often criticized for this, the criticism being that such interests were superficial. But surely a man's choice of clothes is as important, novelistically, as his accent or choice of vocabulary.

Yet O'Hara was not alone among modern novelists in being interested in his characters' dress. F. Scott Fitzgerald shared this interest. Mary McCarthy's best-known story is "The Man in the Brooks Brothers Shirt." Saul Bellow, in his story "A Father-To-Be," gets a good deal of fictional wear out of this bit of haberdashery in prose:

> Meanwhile, he had not interrupted his examination of the passengers and had fallen into a study of the man next to him. This was a man whom he had never in his life seen before but with whom he

now suddenly felt linked through all existence. . . .
The coat he wore was a fairly expensive blue check
such as Rogin would never have chosen for himself. He would not have worn blue suede shoes,
either, or such a faultless hat, a cumbersome felt
animal of a hat encircled by a high, fat ribbon.
There are all kinds of dandies, not all of them are
of the flaunting kind; some are dandies of respect-
ability, and Rogin's fellow passenger was one of
these. . . . Wearing such blue suede shoes, he could
not afford to have people treading on his feet, and
he seemed to draw about himself a circle of privi-
lege, notifying all others to mind their own business and let him read his paper.

Increasingly nowadays characters in fiction are unclothed,
rather like mannequins in shops awaiting a window dresser,
and novels and stories are not better for it.

Dickens, himself a triple-crown clotheshorse, in *Martin
Chuzzlewit* has Mark Tapley say: "Any man may be in good
spirits and good temper when he's well dressed. There ain't
much credit in that." I agree. Although I think myself a man
who, in some rough way, lives the life of the mind, I am
regularly surprised to discover how, over the years, certain
items of apparel have lifted my spirits. I have owned
neckties that, when I wore them, allowed me to convince
myself I was witty. As a boy tennis player I had a pair of tan
Fred Perry tennis shorts that—you will have to take my
word on this—gave my second serve an added hop it did not
have in Wilson or Spaulding shorts. I once bought a rain-
coat—brand name Mackintosh, place of purchase Aber-
crombie & Fitch—that, whenever I put it on, filled me with
energy and ambition. Unfortunately the company ceased to
make it, else I should doubtless be writing this column from
my office in the United States Senate building.

Fashions in men's clothes, alas, change nearly as often as
in women's. Leaving well enough alone is evidently a sentiment no designer of clothes finds tolerable. Epaulets must

be put on what were once one's favorite shirts; tuxedos must be made out of the fabric called double-knit; collars and colors of raincoats must be altered to look worse. Not long ago, invited to a black-tie dinner and owning no dinner clothes, I went out to rent some. This proved no simple chore. The range of rental possibilities seemed to be between a tuxedo of the kind worn by a member of Desi Arnaz, Sr.'s, old Cuban orchestra and that of a procurer on holiday at the seashore. I finally located a store that rented fairly straight-forward black tuxedos. The manager—the store was one of a chain—said he thought he had what I wanted but he had better call the central store to see if they had my size. "Jake," he said into the phone, "Sid here. I got a 39 regular in the store. We got anything in a Tony Martin for him?"

One might as well try to persuade the tide not to go out as to argue against fashion, which is no less inexorable. "Fashion," as Gabrielle Chanel said, "is made to become unfashionable"—by which she meant, of course, that fashion is ever meant to be replaced by newer fashion. Fashion is a kind of dialectic that knows no synthesis; it is all thesis and antithesis. If fashion calls for men to wear their hair long, in time the fashionable in their boredom will begin to cut theirs short. If neckties become luxuriously wide, fashion soon dictates they must be severely narrow; trousers flared, taper them; collars long, shorten them; and so it goes. Some things—loafers, knit ties—come in, go out, and come back in fashion; a few others—blue blazers, cardigan sweaters—never go completely out of fashion. Yet custom in clothes can sometimes stale. Fashion can be insidious. One laughs at bell-bottom trousers, then six months later looks down to discover one is wearing them.

What is noteworthy about the current day is that no single masculine style seems dominant. Jock, rock, hippy, dippy, ivy, jivey—instead of a dominant style, there is this smorgasbord from which, apparently, one takes a bit of this, a bit of that, a bit of the other. The gates opened in the 1960s, in what George Frazier called "the Peacock Revolution," and through them have passed, and continue to pass: Guevara beards, cowboy boots, neck chains, handlebar and other mustachios, purses, safari jackets, Russian leather, T-shirts with jokes imprinted on them, unisex haircuts, white shoes, body shirts worn open to the *pupik*. We are talking here about "lifestyle," as in the Bloomingdale's men's store advertisement that reads, "Burberry, more than a label, a lifestyle." Burberry used to be, doubtless still is, a splendid raincoat. Why does it have to be sold as a lifestyle?

Because, one gathers, lifestyles are what people seem to be in the market for. Unlike a life, a lifestyle, as currently construed, is a thing you can turn in, exchange, swap for another. One result of this shuffling of lifestyles is that you can scarcely tell what people do, or are, by their clothes. A certain pride is sometimes involved in not dressing in a manner that might give away what one does. That young man with long hair and dirty jeans—is he a gas station attendant or an assistant professor? That man with a permanent of tight curls and a Fu Manchu mustache—is he a pit boss in Vegas or a reform rabbi? Perhaps the chief reason why novelists now spend so little time describing their characters' clothes is that clothes are telling less and less about character.

Yet, one might respond, what is the point in having a man's clothes serve as his uniform, a badge that tells you pretty much everything that you need to know about him? Things truly are cooler under the new dispensation, less hierarchical, more egalitarian. James Laver, the historian of dress, would disagree. Laver ends his little book *Modesty in Dress* with a photograph of a young man and woman in similar sweaters, jeans, and haircuts, and with the following threnody: "We, as children of an age which values equality above everything else and calls envy social justice, must congratulate ourselves that all these frivolities [of distinctive and distinguished dress] are no more, that Modesty has

proved finally victorious over its two foes, the Lust of the
Eye and the Pride of Life, that the Socialist Paradise has
been reached at last, and Thorstein Veblen can lie quiet in
his grave."

Many would disagree with James Laver, whose criticism
is chiefly aesthetic. A deeper criticism, though, is possible, a
psychological one. It is that all this male costuming, this
dressing up without regard to one's age, social class, true
outlook, has to do with avoiding the formation of character.
Men once looked upon their lives as works of art. A life was
viewed as having a beginning, a middle, an end; a shape
given it by experience; a tone lent it by life's vicissitudes.
Clothes were part of this, and a man chose his clothes in
accordance with his conception of himself. By his choice of
clothes, and by the way he wore them, one could tell things
about a man; if one were astute, one could tell a great many
things. "This costume," wrote Balzac, after describing the
clothes of Jérôme-Nicolas Séchard in his novel *Lost Illusions*,
"thanks to which the artisan was still manifest behind the
bourgeois, was so suited to his vices and habits, so expressive of his way of life, that he looked as if he had come into
the world fully clad: you could no more have imagined him
without his clothes than you could imagine an onion without its peel." Ellen Moers, in her excellent study, *The Dandy*,
remarks that what so impressed people with the young Max
Beerbohm, who always gave the most scrupulous attention
to his clothes, was that even as an undergraduate at Oxford
he seemed to have "a finished personality."

I suspect the very notion of a finished personality is repugnant to most people today. A "formed character" seems positively alien to the spirit of the age. Rather than be finished
or formed, most people, in the rotting botanical metaphor of
the day, would prefer to keep on "growing." Men may wear
T-shirts that read "I Wanna Be Me," but they appear to wear
the clothes of someone else. If they do not quite seem to
wanna be them, it is far from clear whom they wanna be.

Increasingly, men wear clothes to obscure, rather than re- veal, character. They wear, one might say, their so-called identity crises not so much on, but as part of, their sleeve.

It may well be that one can have either a life or a number of lifestyles, but not both. Many more men than not, or so it seems to me, are choosing lifestyles. One sees them every- where: in office buildings, at movies, in movies and on televi- sion, in one's rearview mirror. Wearing sunglasses, helmets of hot-combed hair, sprayed mustaches, they seem not so much dressed as disguised—possibly above all from themselves. Each time I sight a fresh batch of these dandies askew I recall the first sentence of a story I have always wanted to write, which is perhaps better pressed into service as the last line of this essay. The sentence runs: "At nine o'clock on Tuesday morning, Freddy Kaplan, urgently seeking a change in life- style, checked into University Hospital, where he had made arrangements to have a single sideburn removed."

Sex and the Professors

Make Love Not Knowledge was not one of the slogans of the period from the middle 1960s through the early 1970s, yet reading some of the literature of the period might well lead one to believe otherwise. The academic novel has been with us for a long while, but of late it has taken a new turn. Love affairs between professors, or between a professor and the wife of another faculty member, have not been uncommon in the academic novel—a genre that, given the general quietude of the campus as a setting for fiction, has always had to scratch about fairly vigorously to find the conflict or drama necessary to sustain a longish work of literature. (Why are battles for academic power waged at such a high pitch of intensity? a riddle asks. Because, the answer is, the stakes are so low.) Now a new touch has been supplied: students have been added to the cast of characters in the academic novel. And they have been featured chiefly as lovers—more specifically, as lovers of their professors.

The place now held by the student in academic fiction was, in an earlier version of this kind of writing, held by the visiting writer. The situation, however, was much the same. Into the settled, usually rather stuffy academic atmosphere, the writer—generally a novelist or poet, at any rate an imaginative writer—was inserted. He represented the life of the senses, of the great world, and of art, which in this fiction was opposed to the life of the mind, of the academy, and of intellectual sterility. Inhibitions broke down, repressions were jettisoned, chaos resulted. Wild and woolly, *à la* Dylan Thomas, the poet bedded down the wife of the department chairman; crafty and cunning, *à la* Leslie Fiedler in his own fiction of this sort, the novelist seduced the wife of the overly cerebral young professor. Whatever the variants, the life of the senses won out over the life of the mind, bohemia defeated philistia (academic branch), and the previously intact academic community was left in shambles. The target in such fiction was academic life itself, what was felt to be its stodginess, its self-enclosure, its denial of life's possibilities.

The newer academic novel, in which the student has replaced the visiting writer as catalyst, turns things inward. Although it is still in some sense a novel of manners, the chief impetus behind it is not social criticism but psychological investigation. The student, like the visiting poet or novelist, is the agent of disruption, but he or she is also the occasion for much introspection on the part of the professor-lover, his wife, and the other (shall we say) "grownups" in the novel. In terms of plot, though, the result is often much the same: things break up.

To what end they break up depends upon who is telling the story. In *Other Men's Daughters* Richard G. Stern provides a professor in the biological sciences with a lover who is a young graduate student in Japanese studies. In *The War Between the Tates* Alison Lurie has a professor of political science fall in love with a graduate student in psychology. Mr. Stern's professor finds great, if somewhat complicated, happiness in his student-lover, and the affair involves him in a spiritual renewal of sorts, a revivification, the shucking off of a tired middle-aged outlook for a fresher and more hopeful sense of life's possibilities. "I feel about her," Stern's

Professor Merriwether remarks, "the way Galileo did about the telescope. My feelings for her enlarge my feelings for other things." Miss Lurie's Professor Brian Tate, through his student-lover, meets disorder but in the final analysis very little sorrow. "He did not realize," Miss Lurie writes, "that he had betrayed not only Erica [his wife], but himself; that he had become permanently smaller and more ordinary." It boils down to a matter of novelistic sympathies. Mr. Stern, being a man and a professor, has profound sympathies for his professor; Miss Lurie, being a woman and a professor (and also a wife), has nothing but contumely for her professor. The one man is made larger, the other diminished, by his liaison with a student-lover.

I have picked out—or picked on—two rather better-known instances of fiction having a professor-student love affair theme at their center. *Other Men's Daughters* received excellent reviews, and *The War Between the Tates*, along with excellent reviews, has been a modest best seller. But they are not isolated instances. Some years ago the novelist Alan Lelchuk, in *New American Review*, published a story, "Of Our Time," in which a variation on the theme was wrought. A young professor has a student, a divorced woman with children and a life of considerable chaos, who comes not only into his classroom but into his bed, forcing him to reexamine the aridity of his well-ordered academic life. In *A Single Man*, published some years before this, Christopher Isherwood played a homosexual variant on the theme, set in a California college. More recently, demonstrating that the phenomenon is not wholly an American one, the British writer A. Alvarez, in *Hers*, his first novel, offers a variation on a variant by staging an affair between his heroine and one of her professor-husband's twenty-two-year-old graduate students. A novel about a woman professor who takes undergraduate lovers, if it has not already appeared, is distinctly late. (In John Irving's *The World According to Garp*, a book I have not read, I am told that a female professor takes a third-year male graduate student as lover.) In "The Humanities Building," a poem by Karl Shapiro published in *The New Yorker*, things roll along smoothly enough until Mr. Shapiro, describing his own office in the building, notes that in his "cell I hope and pray / Not to be confronted by / A student with a gun or nervous breakdown / Or a girl who closes the door as she comes in." Do such girls come in often, one is entitled to wonder. About the nature of their business no wonder can be allowed.

Given all this, the question is: Is art, in repeating again and again the theme of the professor sleeping with his students, imitating life? Do professors often sleep with their students? Are professor-student liaisons now rather a commonplace aspect of academic life? If they are, what does this say about the quality of academic life today? And does it, finally, one way or the other, matter?

Well, do professors often sleep with their students? No statistics are available, nor are any likely to be. The evidence, as the behavioral scientists say, is anecdotal. The anecdotes, one may be sure, are juicy indeed.

A professor at a large university, a man who is also one of this country's well-known intellectuals, tells of a graduate student, known to be a lesbian, announcing to him that she and her lover have decided that they would like to have a baby, and that, after surveying the possibilities for genetic inheritance on the campus, have selected him as the best available candidate for the baby's father.

At another university a professor was having an affair with a student whose dissertation he was directing. The dissertation was of inferior quality, and the professor, with his inordinate interest in having it accepted, jumped to its defense. But it proved a defense of the indefensible. The dissertation was turned down, and the professor, though tenured, was advised to leave the university, which he did in a cloud of embarrassment touching everyone involved in the fiasco.

In the office I inhabit at yet another university, some fif-

teen years ago a professor asked an undergraduate to remove her blouse. The girl reported the incident to the university administration, and the professor was fired. The then
dean, evidently a man of some worldliness, remarked: "I
wouldn't have minded so much if he had slept with her. But
asking her to take off her blouse—that's sick!"

A letter arrives from an acquaintance, a professor in his
forties, recently divorced, who has been enjoying the fruits
of his liberation. It is an amiable letter, chatty and breezy,
and toward its close the following sentence crops up: "I
must rush off now to see a lady friend—a graduate student,
quite young and unformed and rather poor in bed—but I do
not shrink from responsibilities."

A moderately diligent researcher, I ask a youngish professor, "Do you think many professors sleep with their students?" He responds: "Do you think many don't?" I ask
another, older professor if professors sleeping with their students presents a problem on his campus. He responds: "If
you talk to faculty wives, it does."

Where there is so much fire, to reverse the old bromide,
must there not be some smoke? In the matter of sex and
professors and their students, perhaps there has always been
some smoke. At certain progressive colleges—Bennington,
say, or Sarah Lawrence—love affairs between professors and
students were once said to be, if not quite traditional, then
not quite uncommon either. Such affairs, incidents, liaisons—terminology, no doubt about it, is a bit of a problem
here—were probably always carried on, in isolated instances, at any number of universities. Love flourishes in an
atmosphere of impossibility; the flames of sexual excitation
are often fanned by high risk. The element of impossibility,
and even more the element of risk, was undoubtedly intrinsic
to such behavior on the part of professors. Caught at it, a
professor risked disgrace, official censure, firing. Are the
same stakes involved today?

First, though, it needs to be said that certain unwritten

laws were traditionally applied to the sexual congress between professors and their students. At most schools, backs
were tactfully turned on the love affairs between younger
faculty men—teaching assistants, for example, and instruc-
tors—and their students, on the sensible premise that such
young men were presumably shopping around for wives. If
an instructor of, say, twenty-four had become involved with
an undergraduate girl of, say, twenty-one—well, there was
something rather natural about that. True, such an entangle-
ment might well bring with it certain "administrative" complications. After all, grading the papers and examinations of
a person one is sleeping with calls for an ethical delicacy
most men do not command. But handled with tact, no great
tumult need—nor frequently, one gathers, did—result. Other
professor-student pairings were also adjudged permissible,
such as a young unmarried professor with even a graduate
student in his own department, providing she was not a
student under his supervision. On the whole, and within the
bounds of a tacitly acknowledged and not unreasonable
decorum, the academic community was not intolerant in
such matters.

In recent academic fiction this decorum is regularly and
rather blithely breached. Mr. Stern's Professor Merriwether
in *Other Men's Daughters* is a married man, in his forties,
and has children. Miss Lurie's Professor Tate in *The War
Between the Tates* is similarly situated: middle aged, married, a family man. The breach is not total, however, since
both men take up with graduate students. The academic
novel has not yet, one might conclude, taken a Lolitaesque
turn. Yet, though the student figure in each novel is a graduate student, both of them, like all representatives of the
counter-culture, seem to be a perennial nineteen. Although
Mr. Stern's professor goes off with his student-lover, and
Miss Lurie's professor leaves his behind, neither young
woman at any time seems in any convincing way a victim,
or even in much danger of becoming one. If victims there be

in these novels, then they are the professors' wives. Certainly
they are not the jean-clad, pot-puffing students, who were
sexually sophisticated before they came to graduate school.
"You cannot seduce anyone," Elizabeth Hardwick remarks
in her book *Seduction and Betrayal*, "when innocence is not a
value."

The consequences of Miss Hardwick's remark, for literature as for life, are radical indeed. Imagine how differently
certain literary classics might have been resolved if set in
today's sexual ambiance. *Romeo and Juliet* need not have
ended so tragically if the two families had somehow agreed,
as they might today, to allow the kids to live together for a
while; their passion might soon have been spent, and before
long the whole thing might have blown over. As for Anna
and Aleksey Aleksandrovich Karenin, the solution to their
problems is evident—what was called for, clearly, was an
"open marriage." Finally, had the legislation for legalized
abortion only come through early enough, Clyde Griffiths of
An American Tragedy, instead of dying in the electric chair,
might now be living with his wife, the former Sondra
Finchley, in Fort Lauderdale as the retired chairman of the
board of the Finchley factory in Lycurgus—and Theodore
Dreiser would have had to come up with another title.

To return from letters to life, imagine a hypothetical case.
Assume a professor at a moderately large university has had
an affair with a student, an undergraduate, that he, the professor, chooses to break off. The student returns to her home
for the Thanksgiving holiday in a state of shakiest depres-
sion. She takes to her room, she weeps, she comes down to
meals morose and with red-rimmed eyes. When her parents
inquire what has gone wrong, she breaks down and tells
them of her affair with Professor Smith. Her father decides
not to be philosophical about it. He doesn't find it amusing
to expend some $8,000 annually for his daughter's education
only to have her sleep with a man twenty years her senior,
someone roughly his own age. He returns with his daughter

to her campus, bursts into the chief administrative dean's office, and demands that Professor Smith be fired. What is likely to happen?

Twenty-five, perhaps even twenty, years ago there could not have been much doubt about the conclusion of such a proceeding. Out went the professor, fired (as the common accompanying adverb had it) summarily. Then sex scandals were unforgivable. Professors could be dismissed for overexplicit discussion of sexual matters, even in biology courses. Preaching free love was dangerous enough; practicing it unthinkable. A famous literary scholar is said to have committed suicide after it was revealed that he had received homosexual pornography through the mails. Thus it was—then. Now, at most universities no one can predict with confidence what scene might ensue in our hypothetical dean's office. Would the angry father be placated and promised that appropriate measures would be taken? Would Professor Smith be called in, apprised of the situation, and goodhumoredly requested to cool it? Possibly. But who really knows? In neither *Other Men's Daughters* nor *The War Between the Tates* does fear of official censure from the university play any part; the university's view is, quite simply, of no interest.

A number of objections might be raised to the hypothetical case of Professor Smith and the undergraduate—all of them on the grounds of its unlikelihood. The most interesting, perhaps, is that such an affair is likely to have more significance for the professor than for his student. He, in this view, is much more likely to be left bereft than she. His family, his sexual pride, his hopes of regaining youth—these things and more are on the line for the professor. For the student, the reasoning here runs, all that is involved is an interesting interlude. (Such, once again, is borne out in the depictions of professor-student love affairs in *Other Men's Daughters* and *The War Between the Tates*.) But this objection assumes, of course, that students nowadays, along with being callow about personal relationships, are utterly casual about sex. Is this a fair assumption?

We are all great Kremlinologists of the young today: experts on what they are thinking, theorists on their values, researchers into their psyches. We are Kremlinologists in the sense that we view the objects of our study as essentially threatening, and we work on slender evidence. While we all harbor our private notions, we also take what outside expert help we can get. From Daniel Yankelovich, president of the public opinion firm that bears his name, we get the following in his book, *The New Morality: A Profile of American Youth in the 70's*. In the late 1960s "a new code of sexual morality, centering on greater acceptance of casual premarital sex, abortions, homosexuality, and extramarital relations is confined to a minority of college students," but now, in the 1970s, "the new sexual morality spreads both to mainstream and working-class youth." This is based on "3,522 one-to-two-hour personal interviews" with students, conducted by the Yankelovich firm. When I read the supporting documentation for such findings, I always wish the pollsters had talked to a 3,523rd student, who might have set them straight and caused them to cancel the entire poll. But let us assume for the moment the correctness of Yankelovich's conclusion, that the new sexual morality, the new sexual casuality as it might better be termed, really is now widespread among students. Does this mean that the professoriat, or at least that portion of it that becomes sexually entangled with students, is free from any possible charge of corruption?

I do not think it means anything of the kind. But the charge of corruption needs to be more carefully made. It is not the young, their students, that such professors are corrupting, but themselves and academic life generally. How? And in what ways?

In a handsomely wrought essay entitled "On Teaching Politics Today," Werner J. Dannhauser remarks on the physical aspects of teaching: "I lecture to hundreds, and my practical eye roams freely and fiercely over bosom after bosom. I fix my tie, briskly enter a seminar room, rejoicing at beauty, regretting homeliness—in both sexes—because teaching is a profoundly erotic activity." Professor Dannhauser is quite correct about the erotic element in teaching, and Socrates before him would have agreed, but what he does not add, because it is beyond the boundaries of his essay to do so, is that the teacher himself is a figure of eros, in all the multi-various meanings of that word. There the teacher stands, behind the lectern or at the head of the seminar table, the man with the most knowledge in a room where knowledge is the only business of the hour, a figure of authority, confidence, intellectual grace—an object, if he does his work even half-well, of love. In the close and charged atmosphere of the classroom, he is a guide, an older brother, a performer, a father-figure, a lover, wrapped into one. Given all this, no wonder the schoolgirl's crush on her professor is a tradition of such long standing.

In the classroom the professor commands. Intellectually, he has all the moves. If he knows his job, he can shimmer with elegance, shine with wit. He travels on steady ground where the earth beneath everyone else is shaky; he is sure-footed where everyone else steps tentatively. In a roomful of William Bendixes, he is Fred Astaire. He leads; they, his students, follow. He has, in a word, power, and power can be sexy. In a coarse reading of the situation, knowledge is power is sex. Among the professoriat there are evidently coarse readers, men who are not above cashing in on their power in the currency of sex with their students. This is not merely aesthetically displeasing—an instance of Beauty and the Beast—but ethically ugly. Even in the harsh ethics of seduction, the guns are too heavily loaded in the professor's favor. Even assuming that sex is of little importance to the liberated young, professor-student sex nonetheless offends one's sense of fairness.

Still, assigning such a high-blown motivation as the acting-out of power relationships to professors who sleep with their students may miss the mark. Possibly the motivation for professors who do so is no different from the motivation of mountain climbers who attempt Everest—they do it simply because it is there. But in another sense the phenomenon of professor-student sex is the all-too-logical outcome of much that has been going on in the university in recent years.

Largely as a result of the political upheavals visited upon the university in the late sixties and early seventies, the campus has been much democratized. Distinctions between teachers and students have been blurred; confidence in once firmly established hierarchies is shot. An atmosphere of chummy togetherness now reigns—an atmosphere fostered, it should be noted, at least as much by professors as by their students. Increasingly the distance between professor and student has been foreshortened: in dress, in manners, in values. At times it is difficult to tell the players apart without a program, or a faculty directory. In the process, teaching has become less a true calling and more just another job.

Joined to the democratization of university life has been the general worship of youth, which, though initially linked with the political movements of the young, appears to continue unabated. If the worship of youth be a minor religion, professors are privileged to genuflect at the shrine, being located at Delphi itself, where they are allowed to consult the oracle daily. To work among the young is to be ceaselessly reminded of one's own inexorable aging—a reminder that, nowadays, aging begins to set in at around age thirty. With democratization no longer barring easy congress between professors and students, with youth being so ready to hand as an object of worship, the stage is nearly set for the consummation once so devoutly to be avoided: the joining together, the final blurring, of professors and students in the bed.

The curtain and backdrop for this elaborate production has been the enormous amount of attention devoted to the subject of sex in the world at large. As revolutions go, the sexual revolution may be unique in having achieved its final stage so early on. In the sexual revolution, the dictatorship of the proletariat is established, with only a single qualification—it has proletarianized us all. With Masters and Johnson our Marx and Engels, with Drs. David Reuben and Alex Comfort our Lenin and Trotsky, we bravely march (though that is not quite the precise verb) into the future.

Sex is in the air, at the door, in the woodwork, and not least in the university, where it has had no trouble permeating what once used to be described as that institution's "splendid isolation." Few could be found today to argue that the university is especially isolated, or for that matter particularly splendid. Fewer would be prepared to argue that the university has been impermeable to the impact of the sexual revolution. (To make an omelet in the sexual revolution you have to not only break some eggs, but scramble plenty of values along with them.) Divorce does not appear to be less common within the university than outside it. Philandering, emergence from various closets, liberations of all sorts are scarcely even noteworthy in university life. In matters sexual, the principal difference between the university and the blowsiest suburban community is that in the former there is more time available to devote to the sexual life and greater opportunities for its exercise.

In the phenomenon of professors sleeping with their students, the idea of academic freedom takes on a wholly new, and hitherto unimagined, dimension. The freedom involved is that of being no better than anyone else—no more swinish, to be sure, but, should the opportunity present itself, no less. John W. Aldridge, the literary critic, in reviewing Alison Lurie's *The War Between the Tates*, makes much the same point: academic life has been leveled to where it has become virtually indistinguishable from the life of society in general. Mr. Aldridge notes that over the past two decades the realities of life in the university have radically changed.

Particularly among younger faculty members it is possible to identify a new personality style characterized by a nervous, ingratiating gentility, a seemingly cultivated limpness of manner, a carelessness of speech and dress, an air of humility and apology, that inside or outside the classroom might identify them with equal justice as Madison Avenue executives, television newscasters, junior State Department officials, or, for that matter, junior shoe clerks. Their pretension is, if anything, their complete lack of pretension. Their self-delusion derives not from a belief that they are consecrated to a special calling and are therefore above the temptations that beset ordinary men, but rather that they are no different from anybody else, have no wish to be, and would be satisfied if they could be left alone to pursue the modest pleasures of being ordinary.

Faculty-student sex, in this reading, is essentially another way for professors to assert their ordinariness, which is true but which is also a criticism grounded in snobbery.

But more than a breach of taste, a question of snobbery, is involved. However widespread faculty-student sex may be—and it is worth repeating here that no one knows how widespread it is—certainly it is not epidemic. Among those professors who do not go in for it, and choose to adduce a principled reason why they do not, the reason they offer is that it is "unprofessional." Whatever can they mean? In normal times one mightn't have to ask. But these are not normal times. Not when the *New York Times* carries a headline reading "Sex with Patients Denied by Doctors." Not when a book such as Erica Jong's *Fear of Flying* vaunts sleeping with psychiatrists. Not when a better novelist, John Updike, sets at the center of his novel *A Month of Sundays* an oversexed minister. When professors say they do not sleep with their students because it is unprofessional, they mean to imply that to do so is humanly untidy, that it creates a needless mess which can only get in the way of the main job. Perhaps what they really mean is that they do not do so because they fear the stigma of immorality; but they say it is unprofessional because they fear equally the stigma of seeming moral. Faculty-student sex is unprofessional, but it is also wrong.

Aiming high, let us consult Socrates on the subject. Specifically, let us consult the *Symposium*, the dialogue about love. It does not seem perverse to suggest that it is also a dialogue about teaching, which is a form of love, at least as Socrates envisions it in the dialogue. At the end of the *Symposium*, it will be recalled, Alcibiades enters, rowdy and "bottled," as Michael Joyce's delightful translation has it, and, joining the other symposiasts, rather than talk about love, delivers a eulogy to Socrates. In the midst of his eulogy, Alcibiades recounts the most extraordinary anecdote about his attempt to seduce Socrates, an incident curious in itself since he, Alcibiades, was as renowned for his beauty as Socrates was renowned for his ugliness.

Alcibiades took great care in setting things up. He and Socrates went off to the gymnasium together to wrestle and exercise. But it was no go. In an interesting reversal of roles he invited Socrates to dinner, "as if I were the lover trying to seduce his beloved, instead of the other way round." But Socrates left directly after the meal. Alcibiades invited Socrates back again, this time making sure to delay him until a sufficiently late hour so that he could press him to stay the night, which Socrates agreed to do, making a bed for himself on the couch. Later in the night, after the servants had gone off, Alcibiades made his pitch. Socrates heard him out, then said: "And if you're trying to barter your own beauty for the beauty you have found in me, you're driving a very hard bargain, let me tell you. You're trying to exchange the semblance of beauty for the thing itself. . . . But you know, my dear fellow, you really must be careful. Suppose you're making a mistake, and I'm not worth anything at all."

Having made his pitch, Alcibiades next made his move. He

wrapped his cloak round Socrates, and, mounting the couch, crept under Socrates' shabby old mantle, taking the older man in his arms. Whereupon—absolutely nothing happened. As Alcibiades told it to the symposiasts: "When I got up next morning, I had no more *slept* with Socrates, within the meaning of the act, than if he'd been my father or an elder brother."

High-blown and poetic interpretations of this anecdote are certainly possible, but at its most obvious level its meaning is clear: the relationship of teacher and student transcends fleshly transaction, is indeed incompatible with it, being a relationship of love but of love that has to do, as Socrates puts it earlier in the dialogue, with "procreancy of the spirit." It is the first and last word on the subject. Its lesson for professors is beyond mistaking—emulate Socrates or join the Gadarene.

Running and Other Vices

Whenever I see someone jogging by, body glistening with sweat, face contorted with pain, I think of a fellow with whom I went to high school, one Taxicab Rabinowitz by name. Rabinowitz earned his vehicular sobriquet, as W. C. Fields might have put it, from traveling almost exclusively by cab. I did not know him well, but on those occasions when I did see the Cab, as intimates called him, he inevitably appeared to be either emerging from or entering into yet another taxicab. Taxicab Rabinowitz was one of those boys who go directly from early childhood to middle age without ever stopping at youth. I imagine he began shaving around the age of nine. He wore pointed-toed shoes with alligator trim. He was wide in the flanks, soft in the middle; the omnipresent cigarette on his lip—a Pall Mall, unfiltered, if memory serves—was as much a part of his physiognomy as his well-pomaded hair. Taxicab Rabinowitz was of course unthinkable in a gym suit or athletic togs of any kind, with the exception of a checkered suit to be worn at the track. He was, with his cabs and cigarettes and puffy body, the very antithesis of all that is implied by the phrase "in shape."

"In shape?" I can easily hear Rabinowitz asking. "In

shape for what?" That is not a bad question, to which I shall return presently, but first I want to say that the reason I think of Taxicab Rabinowitz whenever I see a jogger is that he, the Cab, is the last man in the world I can imagine jogging. Miami Beach, Las Vegas, Palm Springs, whichever pleasure spa Taxicab Rabinowitz now inhabits, he is surely not running around it but is much more likely to be seated— most probably in the back of a cab, from where he must long ago have concluded that cab meters, not human beings, are for running.

If Taxicab Rabinowitz is the last man in the world I can imagine taking up a regular regimen of running, then I am the next-to-the-last man. I am, if only in the physical realm, too virtuous as it is. Here is my dismal record: I drink, but scarcely ever to excess. I weigh exactly what the weight charts inform me I ought to weigh (the result of avoiding too frequent indulgence in fattening foods, every one of which I love). I play racquetball, usually twice a week. My cholesterol count is where it ought to be; my blood pressure is normal. I have recently quit smoking cigarettes, a habit of more than twenty years' standing. I both retire and rise early. Quite sickening, is it not? Also a bit worrisome. Enjoying such good health has of late caused me to think myself a perfect potential victim for being run over by a school bus. ("He was in his prime, Emily, never sick a day in his life.") But to enter upon a running regimen is more virtuous than even I care to be.

No mistake, it is the virtuousness of runners that appalls— the notion that their running makes them a select breed, an elite of sorts, whose elitism, though anchored in physical activity, goes well beyond the physical. Early last year the *Wall Street Journal* ran an article about people in cars harassing joggers and runners along roadsides: honking at them, spitting at them, nudging them with front bumpers, in some instances running them off the road. The motive, the joggers and runners assumed, was envy of their superior health. Ah, how readily the scene sets itself in the mind! A jogging couple, resplendent in polyester warm-up suits, blond brows aglow with a fine coat of perspiration; then up drives a long Lincoln, one of those gas burners that got us into the energy crisis to begin with; the fat, beetle-browed driver behind the wheel shifts a cigar stub in his jaw, slips the Lincoln out of Cruise-o-matic, and, muttering obscenities, aims his car toward the jogging couple—who embody good health, sensible economy, and (let's face it) everything America could and indeed ought to be.

Implicit in this scene, too, is the notion that joggers and runners are an endangered species of sorts, though few things could be further from the truth. For twenty-six–mile marathon races in Boston, New York, and Chicago, runners turn out by the thousands; soon the mark of a bush-league town will be that it does not have a marathon. Yet marathon runners are but a minuscule portion of people who run noncompetitively: those who run before work in the early morning or after work in the early evening, the weekend runners, and those who run whenever they can. They have become part of the landscape, these joggers and runners, sometimes the first thing one sees out the window in the morning. One sees them chugging alongside the Potomac in Washington, up and down every street and footpath in Eugene, Oregon, at sunup in Manhattan, in middle western parks. Chicago has already had a jogging rapist whose victims have been women jogging in forest preserves. A commonly cited figure for the American running population is twenty-five million.

This surging pedestrianism seems to disregard strict social confines. Running/jogging is not something done chiefly by the upper middle class, nor is it preponderantly suburban. The young go in for it in great numbers, of course, but the middle-aged are padding along with them, and even the quite old are huffing not far behind. Running is unisex at all but the competitive levels, and as many (perhaps more) women as men seem to be swept up by it. Motives for running seem as varied as the backgrounds of runners; among them are wanting to lose weight, gain muscle tone, take fresh air and exercise, feel achievement, extend and test physical capacity. More arcane motives for running, if they were not present to begin with, have since been supplied. Running "highs" are now spoken of. In some of the books about running, not simply exercise but "ecstasy" is held to lie just down the path. In short, the oily fingers of the consciousness movement have taken hold. "Sweat reaches places nothing else reaches," says Dr. George Sheehan, one of the gurus of running. "Sweat cleanses you."

And the purveyors of running gear, one ought quickly to add, pick you even cleaner. Among the advantages of running, one might suppose, is that it would seem to require so little in the way of equipment; shoes, shorts, a road—doesn't that about cover it? Not quite. No sooner had the fad of running begun in earnest than abreast of it trotted up the publishers, manufacturers, merchandisers. These running dogs of capitalism are even now running all the way to the bank. They founded magazines, such as *Runner's World* and *The Runner*, that seek to proselytize even as they preach to the converted. Books in plenty continue to appear: practical manuals like *Guidelines to Successful Jogging, Aerobics for Women, Computerized Running Training Programs*; books holding out hope and promise such as *The Joy of Running* and *Run for Your Life*; biographies of long-distance runners; and books of philosophic purport such as *Running and Being: The Total Experience* (this last by Dr. Sheehan, who has become something of a J. P. Sartre in an athletic supporter).

Riffling through the pages of the new magazines devoted to running, one could conclude from the advertisements that there are more kinds of running shoes now on the market in America than there are feet. But this is not to speak of such auxiliary items as special arch supports, heel protectors, insoles; nor of fog-repellents for glasses, or skin lube to prevent chafing under the arms, or runner's mittens; nor of warm-up suits, singlets, socks, and shorts (one manufacturer sells shorts that he advertises as "almost like running nude"). Then there are metric conversion scales, chronographs and stopwatches, wallets that attach to running shoes, pouches to fit on the back of shorts. One of my favorite items is a "jogging stick," comparable to a military swagger stick, to be carried along while running and to be used, apparently, for beating off dogs, muggers, perhaps smokers.

Ours is an age of health, and the runner is surely our most fanatical seeker after health, a Hasid at the altar of Hygeia. Various explanations have been adduced for the excessive concern with health in our day. The novelist Mary Gordon, for example, feels that it has to do with politics taking a turn inward. Unable to control the external world of events, she explains, we seek to control the internal world of our bodies. "If we can't stop Seabrook," writes Miss Gordon, "maybe we can lengthen our Achilles tendons." There may well be something to this. Others seem to feel that a political profile can be discerned among running folk; as I write, a comedy revue in the Middle West carries the title *Great Jogging Liberals*. But I think something rather more fundamental is entailed. I think it is, at bottom, the fear of death that keeps joggers and runners jogging and running. This seems to me a reasonable enough fear, and one we all share. The only difference between joggers and runners and the rest of us, when it comes to the fear of death, is that they are doing something about it: they are running from it.

Our own age of health has a historical precedent in the early and middle Victorian age in England. The setting for the nineteenth-century concern with health seems to have been rampant sickness and arbitrary death. In *The Healthy Body and Victorian Culture*, Bruce Haley notes: "Nothing occupies a nation's mind with the subject of health like a general contagion." England in the 1830s and 1840s, according to Professor Haley, was lashed by three tidal waves of contagious diseases: "the first, from 1831 to 1833, included two influenza epidemics and the initial appearance of cholera; the second, from 1836 to 1842, encompassed major epidemics of influenza, typhus, smallpox, and scarlet fever; in the third, from 1846 to 1849, there were occurrences of typhus, typhoid, and cholera." As a result of such devastations, the English became health-minded, and the body became a thing to be cultivated as sedulously as the mind—perhaps even more so. In England this was the time of the rise of many sports, among them mountaineering, cycling, lawn tennis, rugby, rowing, badminton, and roller skating. This was the time of the installation of games into the regular life of public schools. (The Battle of Waterloo won on the playing fields of Eton and all that—which, according to Professor Haley's researches, the Duke of Wellington never in fact said.) This was, finally, the time of the rise of what was known as muscular Christianity.

The analogy between the Victorian setting and our own is not altogether tidy, but it does have some things to recommend it. We currently live under no fear of contagion, but every one of us has had to shiver at the black prospects of cancer or heart disease. Much of our concern with diet in recent years is about these grim prospects. We must not choke up the arteries with fat, or send the blood pressure rocketing, or breathe the bad air, or swallow anything on Dr. Nader's Index of Prohibited Foods. ("Whoso speaks on Health," wrote the Victorian G. H. Lewes, "is sure of a large audience"—which might serve as a gloss on Ralph Nader's career.) Like the Victorian age, too, our own has seen an efflorescence of sport, and not alone spectator sport. Over the past decade alone, participants in tennis, skiing, backpacking, racquetball, and jogging and running have all grown hugely in number. In part this growth has had to do with an increase in leisure and a fairly steady level of affluence—what is nowadays considered an acceptable pair of ski boots runs to around $250—but in even greater part it has had to do with our slightly terrified concern about not getting proper exer-

cise, being healthy, staying in shape. If the Victorians went in
for muscular Christianity, we, in our more secular age, appear ready to settle for simple muscularity.

The late Robert Hutchins, when chancellor of the University of Chicago, used to say that whenever he felt like exer-
cising he would lie down till the feeling passed, which inevitably it did quite soon. Hutchins also said that if you have to
watch the meter, don't take a cab. (These two apothegms
ought to qualify him as Taxicab Rabinowitz's man for all
seasons.) But Hutchins's advice had certain limitations. Tall
and slender, absolutely princely in carriage, Robert Hutchins was one of those fortunate creatures who came by his
physical elegance naturally. (He probably also had most of
his cab fares paid by other people or by expense account.)
Hutchins was, it will be remembered, the man who dropped
football from the University of Chicago; implicit in his decision was the idea that the life of the mind need have no
further traffic with the life of the body—once the majoritar-
ian view among intellectuals and academics. Hutchins believed and they believed, along with Montaigne, that it was
sufficient to maintain "the soul and reason in good trim."

In an extraordinary reversal, it now often appears that the
best way to maintain the soul and reason in trim is first to
have the heart and legs and lungs in trim. This, too, is not
altogether new. Professor Haley quotes a character in a
Charles Kingsley novel of 1871: "Believe me, it may be a very
materialist view of things: but fact is fact—the *corpus sanum*
is father to the *mens sana.*" Most regular runners would seem
to hold to this notion. Attend, for example, to James F. Fixx,
author of *The Complete Book of Running*, arguing *against* the
idea of running as a religion:

> It's easy enough to see how running got con-
> fused with religion. Running can, it's true, make
> you imagine yourself a better person than you are.
> Yesterday, I ran for an hour through a seaside
> park near my home in Connecticut. The last of the

leaves were tumbling in the wind. I ran past three
imperturbable skunks, a raccoon, a family of squirrels busily laying in a winter's supplies. A pheasant noisily took to the air at the sound of running
shoes on gravel. By the time I got home, I felt
refreshed and beatified. I know of no human activity, except perhaps sex, that can do so much in so
brief a time, and do it so wonderfully.

Mr. Fixx is a temperate, no doubt altogether reasonable
man. He does not talk about being in touch with the spirit
while running; he does not confuse sweat with salvation.
Neither does he equate modern-day runners with a persecuted religious sect, as I have heard another running maven,
a man named Joel Henning, do. Yet when I read a passage
like Mr. Fixx's above, why do I wish its author, not exactly
ill, but a plague of life's little inconveniences? As he runs
through his seaside park, I hope that he will one day perturb
those three skunks sufficiently for them to loose their most
noxious perfume upon him; that the raccoon will take a
small bite out of his, Mr. Fixx's, running shoe; that the
pheasant who now noisily takes to the air at the sound of
Mr. Fixx's foot on gravel will instead smile at the sound of
the same foot squishing in pheasant droppings.

Quite a little animus I seem to have built up here. Whence
does this animus derive? From, I suspect, Mr. Fixx's and
other runners' avowed self-satisfaction, from their not altogether suppressed smugness. Note, for example, the nudging
reference to sexual activity in Mr. Fixx's last sentence. He is
saying that his running is splendid, no question about it, but
that his sex is even better. This leads one to think that a
jackpot awaits the author of a guidebook to be entitled *Sex
While Running*.

If my animus is strong, it is not solitary. More than one
person has remarked upon the great boringness of running
as a conversational subject. The vanity of the long-distance
runner has become notorious. Tom Wolfe, among his series
of monthly drawings in *Harper's*, has a particularly devastat-

ing drawing of a grotesquely misshapen middle-aged couple running through a Marin-County–like suburb. The drawing is entitled "The Joggers' Prayer," and the prayer reads:

> Almighty God, as we sail with pure aerobic grace and striped orthotic feet past the blind portals of our fellow citizens, past their chuckroast lives and their necrotic cardiovascular systems and rusting hips and slipped discs and desiccated lungs, past their implacable inertia and inability to persevere and rise above the fully pensioned world they live in and to push themselves to the limits of their capacity and achieve the White Moment of slipping through The Wall, borne aloft on one's Third Wind, past their Cruisomatic cars and upholstered lawn mowers and their gummy-sweet children already at work like little fat factories producing arterial plaque, the more quickly to join their parents in their joyless bucket-seat landau ride toward the grave—help us, dear Lord, we beseech Thee, as we sail past this cold-lard desolation, to be big about it.

The smugness of runners, their vanity, may be inherent in the very activity of running itself. Runners chalk up achievement daily, or at least on each day that they run. They have had the body out for a tune-up, a cleaning, an overhaul, whereas the rest of us haven't. Their situation is akin to that of the woman whose car is just out of the car wash or the man who has just had a shoe shine. How grubby, at such moments, everyone else's cars and shoes look! A pity, really. One would think people would have enough self-respect not to let their personal possessions get so run down. A man named Joe Henderson, a consulting editor to *Runner's World*, remarks in that magazine about not missing his daily run in nearly four years: "That's what I'm proudest of: There's something in the way I run that keeps me eager and healthy." Implicit in that sentence is the thought, "And you, Pudge, your *not* running is doubtless what keep you logy and sickly." Reading the writings of runners, listening to them talk, one is reminded of Proust describing Albertine on her first appearance at the beach at Balbec, leading her little band of friends who all had "that mastery over their limbs which comes from perfect bodily condition and a sincere contempt for the rest of humanity."

The contempt of joggers and runners for the rest of humanity is often quite sincere, but I am not sure that it is deserved. Apart from competitive long-distance runners, who tend to be a self-enclosed and solitary lot in a lonely and grueling sport, most joggers and runners are not, at least in my experience and observation, among the best athletes. This may have to do with the fact that running has never been rated very high by serious athletes, other than as a means to an end. Often it has been used by coaches and trainers as a salubrious punishment for such misdeeds as reporting in overweight at the beginning of a season, missing a practice, fouling up in one way or another. Few athletes who have known the pleasure of sport at a fairly high level can content themselves with running as a source of satisfaction in and of itself. Serious athletes understand the need to be in shape, but in shape for something quite palpable: the game that they play. Joggers and runners are people who are content merely to be in shape for its own sake.

The pleasure of jogging and running is rather like that of wearing a fur coat in Texas in August: the true joy comes in being able to take the damn thing off. And because the runner or jogger regards running and jogging as its own end, an element of puritanical fanaticism easily insinuates itself. Thus a writer on the subject named Tom Osler, who does "not wish to be numbered with those who make claims of special life-extending benefits from it [running]," turns out to have run once for twenty-four hours straight, covering a distance of 114 miles (not, surely, everybody's idea of a day well spent). Thus *Runner's World* informs female readers that it is quite all right to run pregnant, right up to the day of delivery. There are people who are now beginning to run up mountains. Soon, doubtless, races will be held in which the contestants will wear lead in their shoes, or carry snow tires in their arms, or strap their accountants on their backs. If it feels good to remove a fur coat in Texas in August, how much better it will feel to remove a fur coat, leather leggings, and a tank helmet in Yucatan.

Committed joggers and runners would dispute all this. As for the argument that others use running as a means to an end while for them it is an end in itself, this they wouldn't concede at all. Running is not merely getting in shape per se; it is, many runners would reply, getting in shape for life. "Since I started running regularly, my outlook is better, my confidence greater, my self-regard higher"—such is the kind of testimonial one finds in the letters columns of the running magazines. Besides, what is the matter with getting in shape per se? Is not good health one of those things worth pursuing as an end in itself?

It is, up to a point. The point is when the concern with good health becomes unseemly—almost, one is tempted to say, unhealthy. The most cheering thing about good health is that it allows one not to think about one's health. Think too closely about it, dwell on it too long, and, lo, it will depart. Has there ever been a less robust crowd than the customers (and usually the clerks) in health food stores—with their sallow skins, dull eyes, bony carcasses, the human equivalent of horses ready to be shipped off to the glue factory? Joggers and runners, though they look rather better, are similarly preoccupied, even obsessed, with their bodies. "I eat bread sparingly," writes Tom Osler. "In the summer, I consume large quantities of fruit juices. . . . I do not use salt at the table or at the stove. I do not use sugar, because it seems to make my skin break out in acne." In an article titled "Running Through Pregnancy" in *Runner's World*, we learn that runners "have little trouble with irregularity. Some even experience a frequency increase in bowel movements." In the pages of the same magazine Joe Henderson reports that he thinks of a running high "as the way we're supposed to feel when not constipated." If one did not know what was being talked about—running—one might feel like an eavesdropper listening in on conversations in a nursing home for the elderly.

As it turns out, many joggers and runners do seem to require a certain amount of nursing, and the precise benefits of jogging and running are very much in the flux of controversy. As nearly as I can make out, internists appear to think jogging/running quite a good thing for circulation, respiration, general metabolism. Orthopedists, bone and joint men, appear to deplore it, citing its potential for injury: shin splints, stone bruises, tendonitis of the knee or ankle, spinal troubles. All physicians agree that great care must be taken, especially if one is past forty years old, when too strenuous a running program can be dangerous. To die from a heart attack while jogging seems neither a glorious nor a philosophical death. The French used to speak of dying as "stumbling into eternity," which seems to me far preferable to running toward the same destination.

While runners come from a diversity of backgrounds, there is much to unite them. An article in *The Runner* puts it thus: "The enemy lines are drawn. Divergent lifestyles foster a see-saw phenomenon. One side must be put down for the other to go up: smoker versus non-smoker, vegetarian versus meat-eater, runner versus non-runner." If ever two groups were opposed, surely these two groups are runners and smokers. Running is one of the few things that cannot be done while smoking, and smoking is one of the chief things runners despise. The same article in *The Runner* notes that "a lot of runners are extremely obnoxious about that [smoking]. They're pompous. They're rude. They go and take a cigarette out of someone's hand."

Yet why, pressed to a hasty generalization, do I tend to prefer the company of smokers over that of runners? The most obvious reason is that smokers are not always talking about their smoking and their bad health in the way runners, when not on crutches, tend to talk about their running and good health. Smokers as a group tend therefore to be rather less boring than runners. But the reasons, I think, go deeper.

Although Robert Coles has not yet written a book about them, smokers are today something of a persecuted minority in the United States. A friend who works in a large corporation reports to me that at least one department head there refuses to hire smokers because other people in the department stridently complain about the smoke. States and municipalities have of late held referendums—and some have put laws upon the books—outlawing smoking in public places. We may one day be headed for a new Volstead Act prohibiting smoking. Smokers meanwhile have come to take on the hesitant manners of the persecuted. "Do you mind if I smoke?" once the most perfunctory of questions, is perfunctory no longer. "Damn right I mind, buddy!" can come shooting back in response.

"The exquisite vice," as Oscar Wilde called smoking cigarettes, has become the nasty habit. Where once the cigarette was an accoutrement of elegance—think of André Malraux, Humphrey Bogart, Franklin Delano Roosevelt, all of whom could almost be said to have worn cigarettes, and worn them very well—the cigarette has now become a mark of enslavement to a shameful practice. "God gave us tobacco to quiet our passions and soothe our grief," says a character in Balzac. But no longer. Nowadays it is said that around 80 percent of all smokers would like to be able to quit.

That roughly 100,000 of the 390,000 annual deaths owed to cancer can be linked to smoking, that smoking is a great stimulus to heart attack, that it reduces sexual appetite in men, that some 37,000,000 people will shorten their lives because of smoking—none of this would most smokers dispute. As I believed it as a smoker, so do they believe it. The fact is that smoking has nothing to do with belief, or with rationality. But quitting smoking is one of the world's great small nuisances—"Quitting smoking is easy," said Mark Twain, a cigar smoker, "I have done it a thousand times"— so difficult in its way that comparing nicotine addiction with that of alcohol and heroin, while farfetched, is not altogether crazy. Having finally succeeded in stopping smoking after many abortive attempts, I now find that I have exchanged one habit for another, and spend half my waking hours with a hard candy or lozenge in my mouth. I may be one of the first men in history to die of tooth decay.

Yet smoking, and struggling to quit smoking, does give one a keen sense of human imperfectibility. My attempts to quit smoking—so small and mean a thing, as I keep telling myself, to ask of so large and generous an intelligence—long ago killed off the last remaining vestiges of utopianism in me. I do not mean to imply that smoking makes anyone more intelligent. Given all that is known about smoking, it is a supremely unintelligent thing to do. Toward the end of my struggle I found myself smoking less and despising myself more. But this most pertinacious and exasperating habit teaches a healthy regard for human limitation.

Runners, on the other hand, are full of thoughts of human possibility. If one runs seven miles in the spring, perhaps by autumn one can do ten miles. The pages of the running magazines revel in the mention of runners in their seventies and eighties. I have read about a new magazine calling itself *Nutrition Health Review*, which (according to an ad in the magazine *Mother Jones*) asks, "Can You Live to Be 100?" The question is rhetorical, and the answer is that, watching what you eat and imbibe, you can indeed. But why stop at 100? Why not 120, or 150, or 200?

"What!" Frederick the Great is supposed to have said to a general who informed him of his troops' refusal to go into battle, "Do they expect to live forever?" Runners, like all truly self-absorbed perfectibilitarians, do seem to expect to live forever. Perhaps they do not expect to run forever—only up to the age of (say) ninety, at which point many could be got to agree to taper off. "I grow old . . . I grow old . . . / I shall wear the bottoms of my trousers rolled," says J. Alfred Prufrock. But were he a runner, he would doubtless add: "But, look, above my rolled-up trousers I wear the two-toned singlet of tricot from Sport International, which prevents chafing and whose mesh bottom prevents it from clinging, thus helping me keep dry. While below I wear the Wildcat running shoe, from Autry Industries, Inc., whose thick heel and ankle padding helps protect my Achilles tendons." Our new Prufrock shall no longer walk but now run upon the beach / no longer hear the mermaids singing, each to each / but only the pounding of blood in his ears / drowning out thoughts of death and other legitimate fears.

Sinning in Black and White

I have for some time—it must be nearly five years now—been promising to buy a color television set. I talk a good deal about it. I say, "In the spring I'll do it." Then spring comes and goes, and I have not done it. "Maybe in the fall," I say, but fall passes and it is not yet done. "When are the sales on?" I ask. But the sales on color television sets are over, and I am still watching black and white. Why? I purchase other items easily enough: clothes, cars, even houses. What is the problem with purchasing a color television set? I have thought a bit about this, and finally conclude that I cannot do it because I think watching television is a sin. I accept sin—original and unoriginal, and my own most tolerantly of all—but I suppose I feel it is not to be encouraged. If sin one must, better to sin in black and white than in living color.

Of what does the sin of watching television consist? No need to call a meeting of the Sanhedrin to derive the answer. The sin is time-wasting. "Time wasted is a theft from God," noted Amiel in his *Intimate Journal*, and I happen to think Amiel correct. Wasting time is not a very exciting sin, I grant you, not at all enticing in any sense that the Marquis de Sade would comprehend or that Stendhal had in mind when he remarked that the only thing wrong with eating ice cream was that it wasn't a sin. Still, as one grows older, one likes to think that one can make each day count; therefore any day at the end of which, tumbling into bed, one has to note that four to six hours were spent watching television is not a day that counts. Applying the rules of confession (be brief, be blunt, be gone), allow me to unbosom myself by admitting that, although less frequently than formerly, I occasionally put in such days. To mention only socially acceptable televiewing—a ball game of a Sunday afternoon, a session of *Masterpiece Theatre*, the news, an old movie afterward—and there are six hours down (shall we say?) the tube.

To shift from theological to psychological terms, let me quote what I think is the most perceptive single sentence written about watching television. It was written by Martin Mayer and appears in his book *About Television* (1972). The sentence is splendidly un-McLuhanesque: "Watching television is a habit." Now, having read it, you may not hear cannons go off, or see the skies light up, or feel the earth move, but anyone who has logged his hours before a television set will agree that a habit is a precise description of what much television watching is. A habit: a pattern of behavior acquired by frequent repetition of, or exposure to, something, a thing one falls easily into and finds difficult to climb out of. Whether television is a good or bad habit is another question.

For all educated, enlightened, and right-minded people, of course, the question has long been settled. Television is a nasty habit—the mental equivalent of smoking; or, as someone once called it, "chewing gum for the eyes." Consider the names we have for television, for the instrument itself: idiot box, boob tube, rube tube, the haunted aquarium, black-and-white hole of Calcutta. Some years back an almost unknown young man named Newton Minow, at the time chair-

man of the Federal Communications Commission, pronounced television "a vast wasteland." By uttering those
magic words—it was Aladdinish, really—Minow instantly
propelled himself to fame among the educated, enlightened,
and right-minded. A vast wasteland—exactly!

A cartoon in a recent *New Yorker* has a man seated in his
armchair before a television set, the bubble above his head
reading, "To think people are watching this." I know that
man; I think I may be he. The cartoon, in any event, reminds
me of an experience of some years ago, when I worked as the
director of an antipoverty program in the South. Along with
the principal of a local grammar school, a black woman of
middle years, I was taken on a tour of one of the city's bleakest neighborhoods, composed for the most part of small,
shabby bungalows known in the South as shotgun houses.
These houses, more like hovels, had walls covered with tar
paper, more often than not no plumbing, and floor heaters
that turned them into tinderboxes. Yet every house I entered
had a television set, usually in use with a child watching it.
As an educated, enlightened, right-minded person, I remarked upon this, in a tone that might be termed snidely
ironic, to the grammar school principal.

"You will have to excuse me," she said, "but I must disagree with you about those television sets. I say thank God for
them. These children hear so little English spoken at home,
and most of it not very good. The things they see on television may seem so much junk to a university graduate, but
without television many of these children would come to
school even more ill prepared than they are now."

I stood, and stand yet, corrected.

Habit though it be, watching television is a habit with
varying effects. But what these effects are no one seems to
know, at least not with any precision. A good example is
the well-known children's program *Sesame Street*, television's largest educational experiment. *Sesame Street* has indeed improved the educational achievement of children

who have been having difficulties in learning. But it has also improved the educational achievement of bright children, which puts things right back where they were to begin with, and from which one could draw the uninteresting conclusion that one educational testing service did: "Bright children learn more from television. Other things being equal, they learn more from *any* learning experience than less bright children do."

Or, to view the matter from its gloomier side, there is the vexing question of determining how violence on television affects the young. In a notorious incident of recent years an adolescent boy in Florida murdered an aged woman in a way that resembled a story he had seen on *Kojak*, the television detective series. Clear evidence, it would seem—clinching the argument against violence on television. And yet does it? One recalls two only slightly older, if vastly more intelligent, adolescents at the University of Chicago in the 1920s, Leopold and Loeb, who committed an equally heinous murder, taking their scenario from Friedrich Nietzsche. Or, again, consider the banning from television of cigarette commercials—a move which, begun so optimistically, seems to have had no known effect on reducing cigarette smoking or anything else, apart from bringing increased cigarette advertising revenues to magazines. Apparently television is so pervasive in our culture, everywhere reflecting it and a reflection of it, that determining what effects it produces and what produces its effects cannot be—or at least thus far has not been—discovered with any real accuracy.

What is known with accuracy is the market for television: who watches what when; what the boys at the advertising agencies call the "demographics." Something like 98 percent of American homes have television sets, and in some 94 percent of these homes they are turned on at least once a week. According to Martin Mayer's findings in *About Television:* "Children, old folks, low-income families and Negroes watch more television than young-adult upper-income whites."

Sunday night is the most popular time for watching television and Friday night is the least popular. People over fifty watch television more than do others. Football games and old movies capture the best educated and highest income audiences. Oddly and interestingly, Mr. Mayer found that "the audiences drawn by both news and documentaries tend to be slightly below average in both education and income, a fact that always shocks people who have not thought much about television."

What is not very well known, if known at all, is the quality of the viewing, its intensity or passivity. With what intensity do most people watch television? Short of wiring up viewers so as to measure their neurological responses, there is probably no way of knowing. My own highly nonscientific observation is that while even very bright young children can become enraptured by television—especially by good things like the old Marx Brothers or W. C. Fields movies, which television has brought back for a new generation—most television shows do not offer enough to hold the attention of most adults. The majority of adults I know usually do something else while watching television: reading, needlepoint, ironing, their fingernails. Only programs of some substance—of which television provides damnably little—command anything like full attention. Apart from watching the tide go out or staring into a fireplace, perhaps no other form of entertainment has ever been received so passively by its audience as is television.

Some years ago E. B. White wrote an essay, "The Shape of Television," in which he complained that television had a captive audience, especially for its commercials, of a kind unavailable to any other marketing device. (Aside from PBS, television is above all a marketing device; this is the reigning fact about it.) By way of analogy, White cited the advertisements in *The New Yorker*, which he claimed exist in a state of fair competition with the prose published in the magazine. Prose runs up the center columns of most of *The*

New Yorker's pages, flanked on both sides by advertisements. If one loses interest in the prose, one's eye goes to the ads; but if one's interest holds, one scarcely notices the ads. This seems to me a true description of the way people read *The New Yorker*, but I am not sure the analogy is otherwise tidy.

At least in my experience, television itself, commercials as well as programs, is in competition with whatever else one happens to be doing while watching it—including, as frequently happens in my case, reading *The New Yorker*. By far the greatest number of my own hours before the television set are spent watching sports—baseball, football, college and pro basketball, tennis, track, the works. Yet I watch much of it with a magazine or book in hand, and more often than not the magazine or book wins out. I am greatly aided here, of course, by that invention so beneficent to the armchair sports fan, the instant replay. I hear the crowd roar, look up from my reading, and, lo, a moment later the instant replay is repeating the home run ball sailing over the left-field fence, the recovered fumble, or the slam dunk. Commercials, I must say, I scarcely glimpse, unless they are very clever, as indeed some of them are. I have noticed, though, that watching commercials with someone else in the room does leave one feeling slack-jawed stupid in a way that they do not when one is alone and can ignore or curse them freely before returning to one's reading. What can you say to a companion after you have both just witnessed a blonde singer, with megatons of false energy, holding a fried chicken leg aloft and instructing us to put a little "Wessonality" into our cooking?

I sometimes think that the decisive moment in the history of television was when physicians began to announce that it was harmful to eyesight to watch television in the dark. In the dark was precisely how one watched television when it first appeared. During the day, drapes were drawn, blinds blinkered; at night, lights were clicked off. It may have had to do with the novelty of this new invention, but concentrating on television did seem easier then than now. Today concentration seems almost the last thing television calls for, and in many homes it has become a kind of visual Muzak. Light has much to do with this. Would a movie shown in a theater with the lights left on seem different than it does shown in the dark? I suspect it would seem vastly different, concentration on it being less and talk in the audience more. Great numbers of people nowadays watch—if "watch" be the correct word—the *Today Show* while dressing. At least we go to the movies fully clothed.

Having lights on in the room while watching television is significant not only because it allows viewers of television not to have to view television with any care but because, concomitantly, it has helped to lower the standards for most television shows. (Another *New Yorker* cartoon shows a woman on a television screen announcing, "The following is not a program. It's just TV.") These standards are low enough as it is. Yet the television industry, as it calls itself, is full of self-congratulation, and bestows upon itself many honors for its own excellence: Emmys and Peabody Awards and, for television writers, the Humanitas Prize. This last, the Humanitas Prize, is given to prime-time network programs for "humanizing achievements in television." Recently the Humanitas Prize was awarded for a segment of *All in the Family*, for an episode of the show *Family* in which the father resists an opportunity for adultery, and for a dramatization entitled *Special Olympics*. Such, then, are the humanizing achievements in television, and they certainly do not seem like much.

Which leads one to ponder an imponderable question: Are the people who put together television programs doing the best they are able to do? Or are they instead acting on the wisdom that holds that no one ever went broke underestimating the intelligence of the American public, in effect saying, "This junk is good enough for the swine who watch television"? I am not talking about art, difficult enough to produce under the best of circumstances (which television decidedly does not provide), but about entertainment. Why does so much of the fare of television, even allowing for the slackest of standards, seem to fail even as unpretentious entertainment? After nearly thirty years before the black-and-white hole of Calcutta, I can come up with only the following rather skimpy list of television programs that have seemed to me to qualify as good entertainment, programs shown on a regular basis that one looked forward to:

1. Sid Caesar's *Your Show of Shows*
2. *The Honeymooners*
3. *The Mary Tyler Moore Show*
4. *Naked City*
5. *Kukla, Fran, and Ollie*
6. *The Carol Burnett Show*
7. *The Bob Newhart Show*
8. *The Muppets*
9. *The Odd Couple*
10. *The Outsider*

Of this list, *The Odd Couple* was of course derived from Neil Simon's Broadway froth play and *The Outsider*, a private detective series starring an exceptional television actor named Darren McGavin, was canceled after a season or two. Other shows began interestingly but soon faded for becoming too formulaic—*Kojak*, for example, or *The Fugitive*, or *Police Story*. There have been some extraordinary moments: Neil Armstrong striding weightlessly upon the moon, Jack Ruby's killing of Lee Harvey Oswald. There have been some handsomely done specials on wildlife: whales, giraffes, apes. ("Wouldn't this," someone—often I—can be depended upon to say, "be beautiful in color?") People nowadays sometimes refer to the Golden Age of Television, when "live" plays were frequently presented, but my own recollection of those plays—written by Paddy Chayevsky, Gore Vidal, and other middle-brow writers—is that the Brass Age of Television might be a more fitting epithet.

Perhaps the one aspect of television that is not passively received is its presentation of the news. I (and I think others along with me) tend to feel strongly about the figures from whom we take our televised news, and what we feel is for the most part strong dislike. ("I never did care for those TV johnnies," says a character in John Fowles's novel, *Daniel Martin*.) I myself had my first inkling that something was amiss with those TV johnnies years ago when, working on a political magazine to which some television journalists contributed, I noted a wide discrepancy between their performance on camera and their performance on the page. How intelligent they sounded on television from the White House lawn or the General Assembly of the United Nations; how utterly insipid they were in fifteen hundred written words, without the aid of superior enunciation and portentous inflection! The larger their reputation, the less there seemed to be behind it. For years I listened to Eric Sevareid—"Eric Clarified," as a *Laugh In* comedy sketch once portrayed him—drone on about NATO, the Common Market, the Sino-Soviet dispute, without ever being able to perceive in his hundreds of thousands of words the least shred of intellectual penetration, originality, or even point of view. Walter Cronkite, who is perhaps even more revered, has always seemed to me an instance of absolute fluency in the service of complete mindlessness, but then he has a face that only a nation could love. The most journalistically competent among them seems to me to be Mike Wallace, whose calculated belligerency can be amusing when used on the side of one's prejudices but otherwise seems gratingly rude. John Chancellor is the best one can hope for. Barbara Walters I refuse even to speak about.

The local TV johnnies are a pastiche of the national TV johnnies. They seem always to have names like Scott Osborne, never Moishe Moskovitz or Theophilus Moore. I take an interest in their clothes. Where do they get such handsome outercoats to wear when reporting from the scenes of fires, bank robberies, and murders? I also take an interest in their jobs, which seem to me fundamentally inhuman. One moment they, or the so-called anchor men or women among them, are reporting the devastation of a flood, the next they are joking about local bad weather, then moving on to report on starvation in Biafra, then recounting a suburban pie-eating contest—their smiles occasionally freezing between the humorous feature story and the full-blown tragedy. Hordes of these media reporters are in the land; every city of any appreciable size has them—good-looking but not offensively so, articulate but never deep, sometimes elegant but usually empty valises. Ionesco has referred to them as *Speakerines;* I sometimes call them the Medes, as Thucydides called the Persians. They are paid large salaries but risk short tenure; should their ratings drop, they are, like soiled plates in a Chinese restaurant, quietly and quickly removed from the table.

Transience seems to be the natural state of things in television. Everything about it seems ephemeral, unenduring, and, apart from certain performers, so nameless and faceless. Can anyone name a television writer? Has there ever been a good television critic who has stayed with the subject for any length of time? Why does it seem unlikely that there ever will be one? Something there is about television that repels lasting quality. Serious people do not seem to remain in it for long.

Unserious though television seems to be, its consequences, nearly everyone agrees, are serious. Jeremiads of book length are written about it, in which watching television is equated with taking narcotics. Movies such as *Network*, mixing sex and sermonizing, inveigh against it. The reason Johnny can't read, pedagogues and news magazines agree, is that he watches television, which is systematically rendering him and all other children illiterate. Television, in these jeremiads, is also a home wrecker. Because families are watching television, they are not, as the sappier psychologists say (usually over television), "communicating." Yea verily, it is

inciting violence in our streets . . . and so forth. Television is
not merely poor stuff, very poor stuff, but a force for rebarba-
rization, the very stuff of evil.

A convenient summary of the evils of television not long
ago appeared in *Esquire*—that force for good in American
life—in an article by the journalist Richard Reeves entitled
"The Dangers of Television in the Silverman Era." Silverman is Fred Silverman, a television executive who in 1978
became president of the National Broadcasting Company,
after succeeding hugely in pushing up the ratings at the
American Broadcasting Company, where he was president of
the entertainment division. Fred Silverman, it is fairly clear,
is something of a *schlockmeister*, and some of the programs
that raised the ratings for him and ABC are *Charlie's Angels,
Three's Company, Starsky and Hutch, Love Boat, Laverne and
Shirley*, and *Happy Days*—in short, the usual winning combination of sex, sniggering humor, violence, and nostalgia.
What Reeves emphasizes is that Fred Silverman, this merchant of dross, is now the head of the *entire* NBC—entertainment, news, documentaries, the whole shebang. "Hundreds
of years ago," Mr. Reeves writes, "it would have been almost
as if one man controlled most of the printing presses most of
the time."

Although Richard Reeves never actually interviewed Fred
Silverman, who was away in Hawaii when Reeves was preparing his article, he has no compunction about portraying
Silverman as a menace—harder working than most television executives, more ruthless, and a great deal more taste-
less. When Reeves attempted to talk with Silverman's col-
leagues on the phone, he tells us, many hung up on him, or
directed him elsewhere, or failed to show up for appoint-
ments. "I have never sensed such fear," Reeves writes, "not
in the Nixon White House, not in the Central Intelligence
Agency."

The substance of Reeves's article is the trundling out of
clichés. He writes about the passivity of watching television.

He remarks upon how, in Los Angeles, only 39 percent of the people watching television preferred the news to quiz shows, comedies, and old movies (rather higher than I would have thought). He quotes Norman Lear, who has made his ample living producing television shows, saying that television "makes people stagnant." He provides quotations from a Rudolph Arnheim essay of 1935 and from Daniel Boorstin's book *The Image: A Guide to Pseudo-Events in America*. In sum—except for one big point—it is clichés on parade.

The one big point is that some friends of Silverman's (who go nameless) told Reeves, "quite seriously, that Fred Silverman wants to be President of the United States." Reeves mentions this again, rather more obliquely, in the middle of his article. The connection is, or ought to be, clear: Fred Silverman, through the control of television, will one day control the nation. Yes, Fred Silverman—to quote Richard Reeves's last sentence—"Fast Freddie, who's reading history books in Hawaii so he can program the nation after conquering television." There you have it, the most up-to-date American conspiracy theory. Big Brother is no longer watching you; you are watching Big Brother.

Richard Reeves's *Esquire* article resembles nothing so much as the basis for a very poor made-for-television movie. Yet his is not an unusual performance on a subject which is obviously important but about which little is clearly known. Martin Mayer's commonsensical view is much more salubrious, as for example when he writes: "The notion that television can deeply affect individual lives, though still plausible, is very far from proved." One of the things that is so very difficult to prove is what, specifically, is new about the influence of television. Television is accused of encouraging fantasies, but then the movies have always done that—and more powerfully. Television is accused of holding families hostage to its allurements, locked in speechless passivity, but families earlier gathered around the radio, and on nights when certain programs were on—*Fred Allen, Amos 'n' Andy—*

one simply wouldn't think of leaving the house. What may be new is that people today by and large seem to spend more time watching television than they ever did at the movies or listening to the radio. And it may be that this difference in quantity may make a qualitative difference. No one would argue that it does any child any good to watch six or eight hours of television every day.

If television has not been proved to have deeply affected individual lives, it is unarguable that it has affected the culture—and so it affects individuals, as it were, on the rebound. Television has, in this regard, brought an end to the American yokelry; as a result of television, provincialism of a certain kind has been much diminished. Television has unquestionably affected—"infected" is perhaps more accurate—national and local electoral politics, turning them into image politics. Among other things, it seems unlikely that, because of television, we shall ever again have a homely President of the United States. ("Sorry, Mr. Lincoln, but you just don't come across on camera.") The TV johnnies have become very important to politicians, who need them for publicity, which is what gives the TV johnnies themselves such an insufferable air of self-importance. Television may also, in a way hard to pin down, have shortened the national attention span. Connected with this, it has inundated the culture with the spirit of the news magazine, in which everything, no matter how momentous, must be presented punchily and quickly, including all the large and lumpy issues and questions of the day—test-tube birth, divorce, causes of cancer—that are the main grist of television talk shows. As much as anything else, television has created a new kind of celebrity, the person, in Daniel Boorstin's well-known formulation, who is well known for being well known: the talk show regular, the panelist, the lightweight expert. A career such as that of Dr. Joyce Brothers, for example, would be unthinkable without television.

But easily the gravest accusation made against television in its effect on culture is that it is ruining education. Richard Reeves reports that in a test of American high school students more than a third did not know that members of the United States Senate were elected to office, while on another examination an increasing number of thirteen-year-olds knew all about a person's rights when arrested. He lays the blame for this not on teachers but on television, evidently assuming that if children were not watching television they would be reading the Constitution. Television has become a more and more useful scapegoat for teachers, and indeed the entire American educational system.

As for how this works, take prose writing, about which college English teachers complain that their students know nothing. "What on earth are they teaching in the high schools?" college teachers ask. High school teachers meanwhile complain that students come to them without any notion of grammar or the most rudimentary knowledge of language. "What on earth are they teaching in the grammar schools?" high school teachers ask. Grammar school teachers for their part say that they cannot combat the influence of television, because of which children no longer read. So at last we have got to the bottom of the problem. Television—the buck stops there.

In fact, several bucks stop at television. Increased violence in the streets—blame television. No one reads any more—blame television. Families are breaking up—blame television. High culture is being despoiled—blame television. And so on. What a splendid all-purpose explanation television has become! In contemporary life, it has now achieved the standing of a reverse panacea; it has become a cause-all. But is it? Edward Shils, in his essay "Mass Society and Its Culture," argues persuasively that "brutal and mediocre culture is the consequence, not the cause, of developments which are quite independent of the specific properties of mass society." Professor Shils holds that the readiness of teachers and intellectuals to lower their standards is more pernicious than the effects of popular culture of the kind offered on television.

Let us be clear about one thing: some ninety-odd percent of what appears on television is junk. This percentage, moreover, seems to be rising, which I personally resent, for much of recent television has become so unwatchably bad that I shall soon have to search elsewhere for new modes of time-wasting. Radio, in my dimming recollection, was better, except for the coverage of sports. But it will not do to pretend that the mass of people formerly put their time to superior uses and that television, some time in the late 1940s, banished us from Eden. Consult Henry Mayhew, the Victorian author of *London Labour and the London Poor*, where you will find the mass engaged in such self-improving entertainments as cockfighting, bearbaiting, and gin drinking, with an occasional public hanging for comic relief. Ah, before television, those were the days!

Foodstuff and Nonsense

Can too great a fuss be made about food? Fifteen, even ten years ago I should have said that any fuss about food was too great, but I grow older and food has become more important to me. As with all solipsists of literary proclivity, this observation about myself did not take long to bloom into an aphorism about humankind generally. "Food," I announced, first to myself, then to friends, "is the sex of the middle-aged." One friend had the discourtesy to rejoin, "On the contrary, I should have thought sex was the food of the middle-aged." Since a statement and its reverse cannot both be true, my aphorism is in a bit of difficulty. Yet as a character in Cyril Connolly's story "Shade Those Laurels" puts it: "They say that food is a substitute for love. Well, it's certainly a bloody good one."

The marriage of the subjects of food and sex is one of long standing, and I should like herein, if I can, to put them asunder. Others wish to keep them married. No one who has seen the film *Tom Jones* can altogether forget that succulent feast in which food was made a form of foreplay to sex itself. Commonplace it is to suggest that food is often a substitute for sex—and wrong as well as commonplace when one considers the great numbers of people passionately devoted to both. But so regularly are the subjects of food and sex conjoined that it is small wonder that eating has not (not yet, thank God) found its Masters and Johnson. One can see their laboratory now—a gleaming stainless steel kitchen, perhaps, or a clinical row of banquettes—with human guinea pigs, their taste buds wired, bosoms covered with large napkins, masticating away, while in the background cameras hum and electronic machinery clicks out a record of the activity of the salivary glands in their encounter with poached salmon or cassoulet.

Not that the confusion between food and sex is so very difficult to understand. Samuel Butler in his *Notebooks* wrote of eating and all the senses: "They [the senses] are all a kind of eating. They are all touch, and eating is touch carried to the bitter end." (Yet Butler, it is good to report, also jotted in his *Notebooks*, "The only things I should greatly care about if I had more money are a few more country outings and a little more varied and better cooked food; nicer things and more expensive things to eat and drink.") Transient pleasures both, the appetites for food and sex are in varying degrees in us all, but, as K. C. Chang, the editor of a recent volume entitled *Food in Chinese Culture*, argues: "These two activities are quite different. We are, I believe, much closer to our animal base in our sexual endeavors than in our eating habits. Too, the range of variations is infinitely wider in food than in sex."

One has to agree with Professor Chang that food has it over sex for variety. Hedonistically, gustatory possibilities are much broader than copulatory ones. Literarily, reading about food is more interesting than reading about sex. The authors of *The Physiology of Taste* and of *Histoire d'O*, for example, are writers equally obsessed, but how charming is Brillat-Savarin's obsession, how sickening Réage's! Similarly, how delightful it is to hear someone describe a magnificent meal, or comical to hear a botched one described,

whereas listening to the same person describe a seduction is
almost invariably boring, if not repulsive. Perhaps the reason for this is that eating is the more social function, sex the
more personal, and as such eating shows people in a greater
multiplicity of poses, moods, and characters than does sex.
Modern psychologists to the contrary, there is more going on
at table than in bed.

Food is essential to life, as the old Erpi Classroom Films
used to say, but, beyond its role in subsistence, is eating
among life's important activities? In Rose Macaulay's lovely
anthology of quotations, *The Minor Pleasures of Life*, although seven pages are given over to the category "Snacks
Between Meals" and two to "Taverns," eating as a category
has no place in the book. From that I draw the conclusion,
with which I wholly agree, that eating is among, not the
minor, but the major pleasures of life. This is a view shared
by Marguerite Yourcenar's Hadrian, in her novel *Memoirs of
Hadrian*. After speaking of his repugnance at the prospect of
attending yet another banquet in Rome, he remarks:

> Do not do me the injustice to take me for a mere as-
> cetic; an operation which is performed two or three
> times a day, and the purpose of which is to sustain
> life, surely merits all our care. To eat a fruit is to
> welcome into oneself a fair living object, which is
> alien to us but is nourished and protected like us by
> the earth; it is to consume a sacrifice wherein we
> sustain ourselves at the expense of things. I have
> never bitten into a chunk of army bread without
> marveling that this coarse and heavy concoction
> can transform itself into blood and warmth, and
> perhaps into courage. Alas, why does my mind,
> even in its best days, never possess but a particle of
> the assimilative powers of the body?

As for how important eating is, right now I should say
that—judging from the space given to it in the media, the
great number of cookbooks and restaurant guides published
annually, the conversation of friends—it is very nearly topic

number one. Restaurants today are talked about with the kind of excitement that ten years ago was expended on movies. Kitchen technology—blenders, grinders, vegetable steamers, microwave ovens, and the rest—arouses something akin to the interest once reserved for cars. In the Bay Area of California, a popular course is taught in something called "Kitchen Consciousness." The journalist Sara Davidson, in a book entitled *Loose Change,* speaks of one of the early years of her marriage in New York as being the year of "competitive cooking." In the Middle West, a magazine called *Chicago* is a whomping commercial success almost solely because of its rather cheerily optimistic reports on new restaurants. The time may be exactly right to hit the best-seller lists with a detective story about a killer who disposes of his victims in a Cuisinart.

An intense interest in food, the products of sky, sea, and soil, is scarcely new. In China during the Chou civilization (*circa* 1100 to 200 B.C.) cookbooks listed twenty different methods of cooking: "boiling, steaming, roasting, red-cooking, clear-simmering, pot-stewing, stir-frying, deep-frying, shallow-frying, meeting, splashing, plunging, rinsing, cold-mixing, sizzling, salting, pickling, steeping, drying, smoking." (I quote from *Food in Chinese Culture.*) Among the Greeks, Archestratus, a contemporary of Aristotle, composed a gastronomical Baedeker of the ancient world. The Romans were of course famous for their ingenuity in assembling luxurious table fare, and Pliny the Elder, in his *Natural History,* tells of the dish of "Clodius Aesopus, the tragic actor, which was valued at one hundred thousand sesterces, and in which were served nothing but birds that had been remarkable for their song or their imitation of the human voice, and purchased, each of them, at the price of six thousand sesterces; he being induced to this folly by no other pleasure than that in these he might eat the closest imitators of man; never for a moment reflecting that his own immense fortune had been acquired by the advantages of his own voice."

About the French fix on food little new can be added, although it is impossible to resist the temptation to repeat the remark supposed to have been uttered at table by Brillat-Savarin's sister Pierrette, then two months shy of her hundredth birthday: "*Vite, apportez-moi le dessert—je sens que je vais passer!*" Brillat-Savarin (1755–1826), advocate and gastronome—famous for his dictum: "Animals feed; man eats. Only the superior man knows how to eat"—is said to have left life like a guest departing happily from a good dinner, the best possible advertisement for a man who lived for his stomach.

In colonial America, in the South, there was a cult of turtle and terrapin, and Virginia was noted for a dish called "preserve of fowle," a Chinese box of a culinary creation that consisted of a dove inserted into a partridge, the partridge into a guinea hen, the guinea hen into a duck, the duck into a capon, the capon into a goose, and the goose into a peacock or turkey, and the entire extravaganza cut for serving into transverse sections. In late nineteenth-century America, a time when Society was dominated by a generation of *arriviste* capitalists, food provided a fertile field for ostentation. Most notorious in this line were Mrs. Stuyvesant Fish's dinners for dogs and her infamous monkey dinner, at which a pet monkey was seated at the table and introduced as a Corsican prince. More traditional high flyers turned out at such New York shrines of degustation as Rector's, Sherry's, and Delmonico's. The Seelys, the Hydes, the Bradley-Martins gave parties at which as many as three separate meals were served; the famous Bradley-Martin ball was said to have cost $369,200.

Such activities have found their just chronicler in the late Lucius Beebe, himself a very great snob with a taste for all of life's extravagances, including hyperbolic prose. In Beebe's account, in *The Big Spenders*, at these dinner parties there were always "mountains of caviar" and "Niagaras of champagne." He tells the story of James Gordon Bennett, heir to the old *New York Herald*, who one afternoon was unable to get his regular table at his favorite restaurant in Monte Carlo. To expedite matters he simply bought the place (reportedly for $40,000), removed the customers from his accustomed table, finished his lunch of mutton chops, and presented the waiter with the deed to the restaurant as a tip. A fine story is told about Beebe himself. One of his lady friends once informed another that Beebe was soon to go into the hospital for exploratory surgery. "Well," the other is said to have replied, "I do hope the doctors have the good grace to open Lucius at room temperature."

Snobbery is of course the fly in the soup of gastronomy. Often it has its natural antidote in the jolt back into quotidian reality, as in the joke about the two ultra-refined ladies dining in a greasy-spoon restaurant, one of whom asked to see the sommelier and was told by the waiter, "Lady, if it's not on the menu, we ain't got it." The snobbery of a Lucius Beebe is somehow defensible in its gaudiness and comedy. But a new snobbery is now on the march. As cookery was once the province of the peasant and servant class, and gourmandising that of the aristocracy and upper bourgeoisie, so now both the preparing and eating of artfully cooked food have come to be taken up by the middle classes in America—and in a big way. As a result, eating, once and still a pleasure, is fraught with a certain element of anxiousness. Expertise in preparing food and the art of eating it knowledgeably are now great status symbols in the United States. Food has become a way of separating *cognoscenti* from barbarians. By their palates shall ye know them. It's enough to give everyone a nervous stomach.

Where there is so much anxiety, snobbery commands the field—and snobbery of a kind that is not redeemed by either grandeur or good humor. An example of this snobbery at its worst can be found, at novel length, in Mary McCarthy's *Birds of America*. Published in 1971, Miss McCarthy's novel is egregiously wrong in its sociology, as befits a novelist who writes about America from a desk in Paris. Precisely at the time when hostesses began to suffer nervous breakdowns over whether to serve Bibb lettuce or romaine, when one most risked being impaled on a fondue fork at the homes of friends, when Hammacher Schlemmer sold vest-pocket pepper mills, Miss McCarthy wrote a novel whose gravamen is that Americans do not care about food. "You don't get the picture, Mother," one of the characters in *Birds of America* announces. "You're out of touch. Americans have stopped cooking." Culinary grievance is piled upon gastronomic horror in the novel's pages: no bean pots in the stores; no jelly glasses either; no fish not already filleted; no plain yogurt, just flavors; no pastry flour; no salted codfish, only frozen codfish in cakes; only instant tapioca. In one scene in the novel we are led to the conclusion that even jailhouse food is not what it once was: the hamburgers—*horrible dictu!*—have ketchup on them. The way one can tell the villains in *Birds of America* is that they eat poorly: not vile stews and filthy hashes, but canned hams and instant mixes. They also rely on electrical appliances. (Interestingly, Elizabeth David, the excellent English food writer, has said that the best possible bread box is the freezer.) A heavy political seasoning went into the making of *Birds of America*, and part of the justification for its concern with foodstuffs is to make the dubious point that people who do not care about the natural in food, such as Americans, soon find themselves committing unnatural acts of aggression, such as Vietnam. Miss McCarthy's message, then, appears to be "Make soup—not war!"

Snobbery about food on the Left is no less common than on the Right, although a bit more unseemly. In the 1930s a now forgotten minor writer who was a member of the American Communist party and who used to lunch regularly at the Waldorf, when apprised of what looked to be a contradiction between his public politics and his private tastes, shrugged and replied: "Nonsense! Nothing's too good for us Reds." Not that one has to be political at all to be snobbish about food.

These days snobbery appears to be, at least in my experience, rampant among academics and intellectuals—always assuming that being a snob about food does not preclude being at the same time quite unintelligent about it. Perhaps this stems from the fact that food, though it can be expensive enough, is still within the financial grasp of most of us and is one of the few means of imitating the upper classes available to those whose purses are otherwise shorter than their pretensions. Of bleak memories in this connection I recall a lunch with a publisher's editor who made an extravagant fuss in a French restaurant about the cheese having been left too long in the refrigerator; another lunch with a former principal editor of *Newsweek* who very nearly prostrated himself to gain the attentions of the maître d' in another French restaurant; and a third in which a journalist, demonstrating his multilingualism, several times cried out, *"Henri, encore vodka!"* No doubt about it, French restaurants in America do not bring out the best in people.

The problem with snobbery over food is that, along with being generally unpleasant, it stands in the way of enjoyment and beclouds what is already a sufficiently mysterious subject. The preparation of food, its presentation, its price, the surroundings in which it is eaten, the company with whom one eats it—all are the most subtle, almost mystical, matters. In an essay entitled "Food," Harold Nicolson tells about lunch at the home of an inordinately wealthy and greedy man who served his guests a soup made in a heavy silver cauldron and composed of the following items: the very largest black truffles, scarlet pepper heads from Thessaly, cucumbers from the Ukraine, spices from Bali and Sumatra, locarto beans from Marrakesh, the roots of a palmetto bush, olives from Ithaca, flakes from the flesh of a giant lobster, and, poured simultaneously into the broth, one bottle of Veuve Cliquot and one bottle of Amontillado. The effect of the whole, as Nicolson describes it, was "like some very hot cough-mixture drunk with shrimp paste." Thus the first paradox about food: the whole can be so much less than the sum of its parts; and, its converse in other instances, so much more.

Or consider the presentation of food. G. C. Lichtenberg, the eighteenth-century German physicist and aphorist, wrote: "Coffee drunk out of wine glasses is really miserable stuff, as is meat cut at the table with a pair of scissors. Worst of all, as I once actually saw, is butter spread on a piece of bread with an old though very clean razor." Why is the prospect of cutting one's steak with scissors nearly enough to turn one to vegetarianism? How is it that one host can make a minor work of art of a bacon-lettuce-tomato sandwich, while another can make prime ribs of beef remind one of nothing quite so much as that bloody afternoon at the Little Bighorn?

As with the presentation of food, so with portions. Chinese parents used to instruct their children that it is best to leave the table when 70 percent full; and I must say I commend the wisdom that has gone into deriving that very precise figure, even though I am unable to live up to it. A. J. Liebling, of late lamented memory, once defined a gourmand as someone who likes not only delicacies but plenty of them. Nevertheless there are limits. I shall not soon forget a lugubrious meal shared with a married couple in which a whole chicken was plopped upon each of our plates. Too much of a good thing—better, I suppose, than too much of a bad thing, but still too much. Or consider price. My favorite Mandarin restaurant recently moved from its location in a working-class neighborhood to one in the most expensive area of the city, with a consequent doubling of prices. The chef is the same, the food looks the same, but it no longer tastes so good to me. Cheapness on my part? I do not think so.

It nearly goes without saying that bad company can destroy a meal—as can, in a restaurant, a bad-tempered waiter. Yet am I alone in preferring, when the meal before me is magnificent, that the company not be too scintillating, but

instead comfortable, even somewhat old shoe? As Lyndon
Johnson said in derogation of Gerald Ford that he could not
chew gum and walk at the same time, so neither can I at the
same time give myself over to splendid vittles and wonderful
talk. I can simultaneously read a book and watch television,
type and talk over the telephone, but to take in two heightened pleasures at once—those of excellent food and fine
talk—is something I cannot do well. My tendency is to be
swept up by the talk, and either to swallow my food without
savoring it or let it grow cold on the plate. Too-brilliant talk
does not allow for chewing in the deep silence of reverence.
Apparently what I need is a sign, of the kind put up during
street repairs, to set alongside my plate: MAN EATING.

As for settings, both physical and human, M. F. K. Fisher
has covered this point admirably:

> . . . gastronomical perfection can be reached in
> these combinations: one person dining alone, usu-
> ally upon a couch or a hillside; two people, of no
> matter what sex or age, dining in a good restau-
> rant; six people, of no matter what sex or age, din-
> ing in a good home. . . .
>
> The six should be capable of decent social behav-
> ior: that is, no two of them should be so much in
> love as to bore the others, nor at the opposite ex-
> treme should they be carrying on any sexual or pro-
> fessional feud which could put poison on the plates
> all must eat from. A good combination would be
> one married couple, for warm composure; one less
> firmly established, to add a note of investigation to
> the talk; and two strangers of either sex, upon
> whom the better-acquainted could sharpen their
> questioning wits. . . .
>
> Hunger and fair-to-good health are basic re-
> quirements, for no man stayed by a heavy midaft-
> ernoon snack or gnawed by a gastric ulcer can add
> much to the general well-being.

I have thought a bit about a number of people whom I
should have either liked or decidedly not have liked to have

eaten with. I should like to have eaten with Robin Hood and
the men of Sherwood Forest, or at least in the film version of
Robin Hood in which one of the merry men cries out, "To the
tables, everybody, and stuff yourselves!" I should have very
much liked to dine with Talleyrand, who was a great gastronome and who, being a clever politician besides, would have
been able to warn me, during dinner, of any revolution that
might be forthcoming. A Saturday night dinner with the
Brothers Goncourt would have been to my taste, especially
on an evening when Sainte-Beuve appeared, for his gossip
would provide a delicious dessert. I should have appreciated
an invitation to the banquet in honor of the *douanier* Rousseau, the event at the center of Roger Shattuck's *The Banquet Years*. Breakfast would have been best with George
Sand, who, after a night scribbling away at her desk, at
table slept through the morning meal. Certainly it would be
preferable to breakfasting with the marathon runner Frank
Shorter, whose morning meal on the day of a race includes a
plate of pancakes (with heavy syrup), a plate of spaghetti
and meat sauce, half a dozen chocolate bars, a couple of
sandwiches, and three or four soft drinks. H. L. Mencken I
should have preferred to dine with in a restaurant, for he
cared immensely for good food, knew where it was served,
and called a fine restaurant "one of the greatest of all human
enterprises, one of the most socially useful things." Lunch
with Hemingway, who wrote so wonderfully well about
food, might be nice, but—"Sorry to have to eat and run,
Hem"—I should want to be off before he suggested that we
go over to the gym for a little workout in the ring.

Of great personages with whom I should not have cared to
dine, first among them would be Augustus, especially if his
wife Livia had anything to do with the preparation of the
meal. The fare at the table of Julian the Apostate, noted for
his asceticism—he lived austerely, said his panegyrist Ma-
mertinus, to make life delightful for others—sounds too
humble even for a plebeian like me. Dinner with the older

Tolstoy would be no treat either, particularly during the days when he struggled to hold to his vegetarian regimen; the thought of the great old man grimacing over his gruel while bickering with the long-suffering Countess Tolstoy is enough to kill off the most exuberant appetite. Although a letting up of table manners would certainly be possible, at least according to Milovan Djilas's account, I think I should pass up an invitation to dinner with Stalin. A man I should have adored to eat with anywhere but at his own home, Lamb House, was Henry James. He was a famous diner-out and appreciator of solid fare, but James's own table, as Edith Wharton has recounted, offered lean pickings. "If anyone in a pecuniary difficulty appealed to James for help," Mrs. Wharton noted, "he gave it without counting; but in daily life he was haunted by the spectre of impoverishment, and the dreary pudding or pie of which a quarter or half had been consumed at dinner reappeared on the table the next day with its ravages unrepaired."

While on the subject of those with whom I should not care to dine, I ought to add that I am made extremely edgy when informed that my host or hostess is a "gourmet" cook. Whenever I hear the word "gourmet," in fact, I reach for my Alka-Seltzer. The word invokes all that is most dangerous and pretentious in food: fondues guaranteed to turn one purple as *aubergine*, crêpes suitable for covering infields during rain delays, Grand Marnier soufflés that sink, first in the dish and then in one's stomach, like the *Andrea Doria*. Nor shall I forget the day a professor of my acquaintance brought to my door—gourmet food to go—a large plastic container of bouillabaisse she had whipped up, which had the dark look of prehistoric ooze (I thought I detected something in it move) and for which I thanked her profusely before consigning it, without prayer, to the incinerator.

One observation on vulgarity of taste that has always impressed me is that the only form of vulgarity that truly matters is that which causes people to reject possibly rewarding

experiences. The spirit of adventure is part of the gastronomic personality. I myself only discovered oysters in my
thirties, an event I liken to Bertrand Russell's discovery of
sex at around the same age, for the result was roughly similar: neither of us could ever afterward get enough. Still,
there are experiences and there are experiences, and, in the
gastronomic line, many are worth avoiding. From the gaunt
and pallid faces of the habitués of health-food shops I take
my clue to steer clear of a concentrated diet of natural or
organic foods. Moreover, while it is theoretically possible to
enjoy the whole world on one's fork, not all ethnic foods hold
equal allure. (Has anyone in California yet opened a quaint
little Symbionese restaurant?) Nor do menus planned on the
evolutionary scale have much appeal—beginning, say, with
snails (things that crawl the earth), going on to fish (things
of the sea), thence to fowl (things of the air), and ending
perhaps with a small child of very high I.Q.

Food is too various to formulate dogmas about, but nevertheless the one thing that can spoil a meal, or even discussion of a meal, is the thick sauce of pretentious language.
Discussion of food requires the light yet philosophical touch,
recognition that it is serious and yet comical, reflecting as it
does something of—if one will allow this parboiled potato of a
phrase—the human condition. For those who care about it,
food represents happiness on a plate, palpably there, even
renewable with the onset of fresh hunger, yet like most human happiness all too transient. It requires a certain worldly
wisdom, a point of view, to get all this in proper perspective.

The best American writer about food in our day, in my
view, was A. J. Liebling. As far as I know, Liebling did not
himself cook; nor did he offer any advice about the fabrica-
tion of meals. But if he couldn't dish it out, he sure could
take it. Photographs of Liebling on the dust jackets of his
books show a man resembling an even more overweight
King Farouk, but from within the flesh a very intelligent
face shines out. A practician of the table, Liebling wrote

solely about the enjoyment of food. "The primary requisite
for writing about food," he noted, "is a good appetite." But
the primary criterion for judging good writing about food, I
should say, is that reading such writing makes you hungry.
This Liebling unfailingly did.

In his writing Liebling occasionally made reference to "the
clear-headed voracious man," obviously a thinly veiled autobiographical reference. The only time his own clear head ever
failed him, in my opinion, was in writing about wines, when
he would sometimes fall into the well-worn trap of preciosity:
"a refined but effective understatement of younger cham-
pagnes, which run too much to rhetoric, at best." But he
could be counted upon to redeem himself with his old common sense: "If a wine isn't good it doesn't 'go' with anything,
and if it is it can go in any company." His pages are filled with
useful tips, all of which, in my experience, turn out to be
accurate. Fifty seats is the maximum for a good restaurant is
one such tip; the Armenians, Greeks, and Turks do best with
rice is another. Often he will pass on tips that others gave
him, such as that any restaurant where you see priests eating
with priests, or sporting girls with sporting girls, is bound to
be good. Liebling was a man who could refer to the menu of a
fine restaurant as "a prospectus for bliss."

A. J. Liebling distrusted abstemiousness. "Hitler," he
wrote, "was the archetype of the abstemious man. When the
other krauts saw him drink water in the Beer Hall they
should have known he was not to be trusted." He looked
back to the day when "to be thin at thirty was a handicap in
the world of affairs." He preferred the time when doctors
"recognized that their role was to facilitate gluttony, not
discourage it." His own favorite bedside book was the *Guide
du Gourmand à Paris* (1925 edition). Only once did he attempt to lose weight, by checking in at a Swiss dieting
clinic—an effort that was fated to fail and that he described
as an event unique in his life: "the only time I yielded to the
temptation to give myself pain."

A. J. Liebling died in 1963 at the age of fifty-nine, doubt-less earlier than he had to; doubtless, too, any coroner would have found that the weapon that brought about his death was the fork. Fat man that he was, his life poses the issue of vanity versus the pursuit of pleasure, or at any rate pleasure harmful only to oneself. (Unlike the lecher, the glutton does not need to bring anyone down with him.) More important, his life puts the question whether it is better to live less long but as well as possible, or as long as possible but less well. It is a question, I hasten to add, to which I, for one, never expect to find the answer. Although I regret A. J. Liebling's death more than that of any other journalist who wrote in my lifetime, perhaps it is better that he did not live to learn about cholesterol, carbohydrates, and Dr. Atkins.

One of the crowning ironies of our day is that, just as the interest in food has risen, so has the interest in diet. (At the end of 1977, cover stories for the same weekly issues of *Newsweek* and *Time* were, respectively, "Diet Crazes" and "The Cooking Craze.") That anti-gastronomic word "diet" has put guilt on all our plates, spittle in the fount of one of the greatest human pleasures. Worse news: as we grow older, our physicians tell us, we must eat less food and that more carefully, for if cholesterol or excessive carbohydrates don't get us our plumbing will. "Do I dare to eat a peach?" J. Alfred Prufrock asked. Yes, and a wafer of Ry Krisp, but that's about it, kid. Is there a lesson to be learned in any of this? If so, it comes from paraphrasing another poet: "Gather ye cutlets while ye may...."

Observing the Sabbath

The sun shines through the shutter slats. An eye opens and sights, on the digital clock upon the night table, the numbers 8:12. More than two hours have elapsed beyond the time when one is accustomed to wake. Avarice for time is no less a compulsion than avarice for money, perhaps a greater. How to make up those missing hours? Then, creeping up from the edge of subconsciousness, comes the sweet realization that this is not a regular day at all; and hence the regular rhythms of regular daily living can be relaxed. It is Sunday, blessed Sunday.

Under Christianity, of course, Sunday is literally blessed. The third century *Didascalia Apostolorum* held, "On Sunday be always joyful, for he who is afflicted on Sunday commits a sin." Gibbon reminds us that in 321 A.D. the Emperor Constantine published an edict which "enjoined the solemn observance of Sunday." The Constitution on the Sacred Liturgy (1963) of the Second Vatican Council says: "The Lord's day is the original feast day," and should be observed "as a day of joy and of freedom from work." Yet if Sunday be officially a Christian day, one does not—to work a twist on an old rye bread advertisement—have to be Gentile to love it.

Not that everyone everywhere has loved Sunday. At the beginning of his essay "The Superannuated Man," Charles Lamb speaks of his own gentle reservations about Sunday, his one day free from his job at the countinghouse. "In particular," he wrote, "there is a gloom for me attendant upon a city Sunday, a weight in the air. . . . Those eternal bells depress me. The closed shops repel me." In *Little Dorrit* Dickens has not a single good word for Sunday. "Nothing for the spent toiler to do but to compare the monotony of his six days, think what a weary life he led, and make the best of it—or the worst, according to the probabilities." "Heaven forgive me," says Mr. Arthur Clennam, the Dickens character who thinks these thoughts, "and those who trained me. How I have hated this day!" But then as now Sunday has never had a very good press in England, where, more recently, it has been thought of as *Sunday, Bloody Sunday.*

Sunday has been better thought of in France. One thinks here of languid summer afternoons: of provincial fairs in Flaubert, of the democratic calm of Seurat's "Sunday Afternoon on the Island of La Grande Jatte," of the elegance of aristocratic Sundays along the Guermantes Way. Modern Greece gave us *Never on Sunday*. Although Tolstoy satirized it in *Resurrection*, under the czars church services were held in Russian prisons on Sundays. (In the slave labor camps, Solzhenitsyn notes, "Tolstoy's dream had come true: Prisoners are no longer compelled to attend religious services.") In present-day South Africa, Nadine Gordimer writes: "While white people picnic, Sundays are the most dreadful days of all in Soweto: funerals, the only category of public gathering not banned, have become huge mass meetings where the obsequies of the riot victim being buried are marked by new deaths and fresh wounds as the police attack mourners singing freedom songs and shaking black power salutes."

Fortunately, here in the United States the worst that Sunday has ever brought us is boredom. Yet it has generally been boredom of a rather luxurious kind. In *Origins*, his etymological dictionary, Eric Partridge informs us that the ice-cream sundae doubtless derives from the word Sunday, perhaps because "whereas an ordinary ice-cream was good enough for a weekday, only this special kind was good enough for a Sunday." The specialness of Sunday was, in an America of another day, denoted by dress: by the idea of Sunday clothes. As a child growing up in Oklahoma City, Ralph Ellison has recalled:

> As a kid I remember working it out this way: there was a world in which you wore your every-day clothes on Sunday, and there was a world in which you wore your Sunday clothes every day—I wanted the world in which you wore your Sunday clothes every day. I wanted it because it repre-sented something better, a more exciting and civi-lized and human way of living; a world which came to me through certain scenes of felicity which I encountered in fiction, in the movies, and which I glimpsed sometimes through the windows of great houses on Sunday afternoons when my mother took my brother and me for walks through the wealthy white sections of the city. I know it now for a boy's vague dream of possibility. . . .

Much of the specialness as well as the boredom of Sunday derived from its being the Lord's day. Churchgoing domi-nated Sunday, and among many sects—most commonly in the South—one attended church not only in the morning but yet again after the evening meal. Unless one felt a strong sense of religious calling or a heightened sense of tradition, the strain of boredom could be excruciating—especially among the very young, who, it could be argued, stood most in need of religious instruction and in temperament were least prepared to receive it. But religious boredom—or rather the boredom with religion—was not suffered by the young alone. Not so many years ago, writing about the then intellectually fashionable God Is Dead controversy, Malcolm Muggeridge recalled attending an Anglican church in En-gland. No sooner did the vicar open his mouth to intone the text of that Sunday's sermon, Muggeridge remarked, than God would be gone. But now, he concluded, with fewer and fewer people attending church, there was really scarcely anything else to think about but God.

Although there is almost always talk of revived interest in formal religion in America, perhaps now, with a seriously churchgoing president in office, we shall hear even more talk than usual about religious revival. Yet in such matters numbers seem so much less significant than quality, and it is quality that is so difficult to determine. At a time of scrambled values, no job poses greater awkwardness than the clergyman's. A dear friend of mine, whose father had recently died, decided, after many years' absence, to return to Sunday morning church services at an Episcopal church near her home. She thought the clear and quiet space provided by the church a good place in which to think about her father. She went once; then on the second Sunday the youngish priest offered a prayer "for Patty Hearst and her associates." God, one might say, was gone, and so, on the third Sunday, was my friend.

When clergymen press so for relevance, how much more sensible it seems to choose, along with the heroine of Wallace Stevens's gorgeous poem "Sunday Morning," the "Complacencies of the peignoir, and late coffee and oranges in a sunny chair, and the green freedom of a cockatoo upon a rug. . . ." For reasons that go beyond the graspings of clergymen to discover what is important to their parishioners, Sundays have become increasingly, immitigably, immutably more secular. To pick up on Wallace Stevens again:

> Divinity must live within herself:
> Passions of rain, or moods in falling snow;
> Grievings in loneliness, or unsubdued
> Elations when the forest blooms; gusty
> Emotions on wet roads on autumn nights;
> All pleasures and all pains, remembering
> The bough of summer and the winter branch.
> These are the measures destined for her soul.

Inevitably, our American Sunday has changed—and so drastically as scarcely to seem the same day it once was. How has it changed? Why has it changed? What are the discernible consequences of the change?

The most patent change in the American Sunday is in the fairly recent alteration of commerce, and chiefly that of retailing. Where once stores stayed closed on Sundays, today Sunday has come to be a major shopping day. Blue laws—so termed because commonly ascribed to puritanical bluenoses who wished to tell people what they could and could not do on Sunday—once made such shopping illegal in most states. Sometimes enforced, sometimes not, blue laws provided a strange congeries of impermissible Sunday activities. Under these laws, barbers, for example, could cut hair on Sunday in California, though they were forbidden to do so in Arizona, while in Massachusetts barbers were permitted to shave an aged invalid. Retail sales were fined $100 in Virginia, though the state's smoked and cured hams were excluded from the ban. The advent of the shopping center and of the discount store, both following much of middle-class life out to the suburbs, eventually caused the removal of many of the old blue laws from the books of many of the states. Once the turnstiles were opened, Americans by the millions brushed through them.

I note that Salisbury College in Maryland has instituted something called "Leisure Studies." Do they, I wonder, consider shopping a leisure-time activity? If not, perhaps they should, for not only is much shopping now done on Sunday— some years ago discount stores claimed that as much as 35 percent of their gross sales were made on Sunday—but shopping has become something on the order of a major American sport. Nor is it solely a spectator sport. Along with shopping in shops, the last few years have witnessed the emergence, in rather a widespread way, of the garage sale—or yard, house, or apartment sale—which more often than not takes place on Sunday. Everyman his own Wanamaker.

Here perhaps is the place to insert the standard paragraph on American crassness and materialism. This, though, is something I find myself singularly unable to do. Not only have I pulled my car over to the curb to attend a number of these Sunday sales, but not long ago, before a recent move, I staged a rather successful one of my own. What mystifying events these sales can be! Why, for example, when I stop to inspect the goods at a garage sale at a home that cannot be worth less than a quarter of a million dollars, do I find nothing on sale but ashtrays, old dishes, and worn-out clothes? What possibly can be the point, for people who are clearly beyond such penny economies, in selling an ashtray for 35 cents? One might answer that by not throwing out an ashtray such people were able to acquire a quarter-of-a-million-dollar house in the first place. But I wonder if a more persuasive reason is that such a sale, quite apart from what small profit it may bring in, fills up the day.

Sunday, for some, can be interminable. "Sunday," Dr. Johnson told Boswell, "was a heavy day to me when I was a boy. My mother confined me on that day, and made me read *The Whole Duty of Man.*" Others who find it even heavier include couples whose marriages have gone sour, businessmen with no aptitude for leisure, the familyless and the friendless—such people can testify to the endlessness of Sundays. At the one apartment sale I staged, some of these people, less than serendipitous in their wanderings, had come to the sale, as they will doubtless go to other such sales, not so much with the small greed of the bargain hunter in their hearts as with the hunger of the truly lonely.

Dr. Johnson believed in the strict observance of Sunday. "It should be different," he observed, "from another day. People may walk but not throw stones at birds. There may be relaxation, but there should be no levity." While I have not, to the best of my recollection, thrown stones at birds, I have most certainly violated the Johnsonian stricture against levity. Growing up when I did, in the 1940s, Sunday always began precisely on a note of levity. I refer to the chief interest of children in the Sunday newspapers: the comics, or, as they were sometimes called, the funny papers. In my childhood, my father read these to me; then I recall a local radio show that read the funny papers along with me; and later, with passion for them only slackening in early adolescence, I read them, Sunday and daily, myself. My own children have never consistently read the Sunday funnies—perhaps, having been surfeited by the cartoon offerings of television during the week, they had no hunger for them—but I remember loving them unabashedly.

For me, nowadays, Sunday morning begins with the *New York Times*, which is, as everyone knows, devoid of comics, but not by any means of comedy. As with so many other Americans, I have for some time been a member of the church called the Gray Lady of the Sunday *New York Times*, worshiping at the altar of cultural and current events. As with church, so with the Sunday *New York Times:* a sense of duty is involved, but how pleasant it is on those mornings when one remains in bed. Still, most Sunday mornings one gets through it, not so secretly pleased when there is nothing that requires reading in either the *Magazine* or the *Book Review*. Of late, I note that the *New York Times* has tried to spread Sunday throughout the week, with its special "Weekend" section on Fridays, and, more recently, its "Living Section" on Wednesdays and now "Sports" Mondays, "Science" Tuesdays, and "Home" Thursdays. I gather that these special sections have been a commercial success, resulting in greater circulation on the days when they appear, yet I feel somewhat resentful toward them. Somehow one can accommodate all the added trivia on Sunday, but it does not go down so easily on weekdays—it is, in fact, rather like watching musical comedy at breakfast.

The essence of the current Sunday is that on it we are more tolerant, if not more indulgent, of ourselves. Not so much a letting go as a letting up is involved. For some it takes the form of lying abed, for others of getting out: on tennis courts, ski slopes, lakes, and links. The most disciplined man I know used to allow himself to take Sunday morning off for reading, with no motive but pleasure. Pace everywhere slackens. In cities in summer, older couples seek the beach; younger couples—because both parties work during the week—seek the laundromats. Such rhythm as the day has is barely perceptible. At their best, Sundays are hibernant, digressive, restorative. William James somewhere speaks of the dues that are owed to oneself, the small change of self-indulgence that is necessary to each of us if we are to achieve mental equilibrium, and Sunday seems the day on which these dues are best paid.

One of the chief ways of paying them has been through sport, which, in our time, has grown much more popular through democratization. Such sports as golf and tennis, once almost exclusively the Sunday pastimes of those who could afford to belong to a country club, are now played without bar by anyone who is interested. Something similar can be said of the more exotic—and more costly—sports of skiing and sailing. To walk through large American sporting goods stores—open, almost all of them, on Sunday—is to realize afresh what a wealthy country we are. Apart from the essentially boyish sports of baseball, football, basketball, and hockey, one finds in these stores rifles and rafts, tennis and jogging clothes, 10-speed bicycles, equipment for court sports of all sorts, darts and Frisbees and soccer balls and Ping-Pong tables, and scores of models of different kinds of sneakers. An up-to-date theory of the leisure class in the United States would very nearly have to be a sociological study of the nation, for we are almost all leisure class now.

This is not to speak of more strictly spectator sports, which remain by and large a masculine preoccupation and which can take up a good part of Sunday in almost any season. Going to ball games—football or baseball, major or minor league—has long been an established Sunday outing, as has listening to them over the radio been a traditional Sunday afternoon activity (lapsing, in my experience, into another traditional Sunday afternoon activity: the nap). But with television this has changed, and radically. Viewing sports can now easily fill the day. Not one but two or three pro football games are offered in the autumn and winter; in spring and summer, golf follows baseball or tennis as night follows day. Now divisional play-off baseball games are played on Sunday nights. The motive is clearly commercial—they are scheduled so as not to lose any serious portion of the audience to the pro football games also broadcast on Sunday afternoons—but the break with tradition is complete.

Deeper as well as more general changes have been at work altering the nature of the traditional American Sunday. Not least among these changes has been the gradual, but by now thorough, evolution of American work patterns. For one thing, over roughly the past two decades the American work week has largely gone from a six- to a five-day week; for another, more women, especially wives, have gone to work out in the world. From these two changes all sorts of others have followed.

With two days free, rather than one, the specialness of Sunday has been somewhat diluted. The weekend, in this new scheme of things, looms larger than the Sabbath. With two days off one can make plans, invest enterprise in leisure. Hitting the road in one's recreational vehicle, taking off for a skiing, tennis, or gambling weekend, retreating to one's country cottage—things once only possible to the privileged—are now more widely accessible to the multitudes. As Sunday was once an at-home day, the weekend now frequently provides the reverse possibility: a chance to get away from home.

With more women working at jobs, the weekend, and Sunday as part of it, belongs fully as much to them as to men. When only the men in the household worked, in many homes Sundays were devoted to the ease of men, the breadwinners. For obvious reasons this is no longer so. In how many homes in America is Sunday dinner still the serious event it once was? (In England, more than two centuries ago, Dean Swift complained: "That Luxury and Excess men usually practice upon this Day . . . dividing the time between God and their Bellies, when, after a gluttonous meal, their senses dozed and stupefied, they retire to God's House to sleep out the Afternoon.") Now, working themselves, women can no longer fairly be charged with the responsibility for an elaborate Sunday meal. Two breadwinners in the home has meant, increasingly, more sandwiches.

Along with the Sunday dinner, another Sunday institution that appears to have gone by the board—one that my own generation, now in its forties, may be the last to remember— is the Sunday drive. The idea of a drive as a pleasure in and of itself now seems rather bizarre. Unless one lives in certain attractive rural sections of the country, whatever can be the point of a Sunday drive, for whatever is there to see? Apart from convenience, no delights are to be found on the free-ways, nor any surprises on the franchise-lined Ventura Boulevards of our nation. Since freeways did not then exist, as often as not one used to drive through the city. Although the purpose of the Sunday drive was more lighthearted—its purpose was, simply, a family outing—one of its side benefits was a lesson in sociology, for as one drove through neighborhoods both richer and poorer than one's own, one saw how the other half, or (in the case of middle-class families like my own) the other two halves, lived.

The Sunday drive usually had no greater goal than a longish ride for an ice-cream soda or sundae. Sometimes, though, its destination would be the cemetery. But more often it would be a visit with cousins living in another part of the city. Customs that nowadays seem almost quaint accompanied these visits—bringing along a box of chocolates to the living or planting flowers on the graves of the dead. Visits to the cemetery perplexed and bored me, for death is, I think, perplexing and boring generally to the young. Visits to living relatives I found a pleasure; I had a number of cousins of my age almost all of whom I adored. Death, relocation, estrangement have, over the decades since those days, taken their toll, and I no longer see these cousins. Were I to set out on a Sunday drive today, I am not at all sure in which direction I would head.

Sunday may indeed be fun day, as a commercial for a schlock clothing store in the Middle West has it, but not so long ago it used to be, for better or worse, family day all over America. Nearly everything about it seemed to be organized around the family, and around an extended family at that: children, cousins, bachelor uncles, widowed aunts, grandparents. I say "for better or worse" because many people find it worse. So much family seems to them suffocating, sordid, oppressive in the extreme. When they hear the word Sunday, they reach for their blanket, so as to pull it over their heads; or for their telephones, so as to call their psychoanalysts. Yet it is those people without family who seem to yearn for it most. Is family one of life's pleasures—peace and quiet are two others—that is most earnestly desired when it is absent, almost unbearable when one is immersed in it?

I do not know if this is an emotion universally felt, but I have discovered that I am not alone in feeling what I have come to think of as "Sunday night *triste*," a feeling of the blues that comes upon me dependably each Sunday, roughly at dusk. What does this tinge of sadness signify? Expectations disappointed? A yearning for a time now gone and not ever to be recaptured? Regret for the winding down of another week, during the course of which one achieved (yet again!) less than one had hoped? Sorrowful anticipation of still another week ahead? Or is it—more simply and more persuasively—sadness at the passing of Sunday itself, one of life's minor pleasures that is now once again no less than a full six days off?